FINAL EXAM

*Poems About Teachers
and Their Students*

FINAL EXAM

Poems About Teachers
and Their Students

Edited by J. Barry Koops

Brooks Street Books
Laguna Beach, California

Cover and interior designed by
Allison Hoffman Tosti

ISBN 978-0-578-61753-4

FOR DELIANNE

who is always ready for the next adventure

and for

SARAH, CHRISTOPHER, JEANNIE,
AND GEOFFREY

and your children:

reading to you is as good as life gets.

CONTENTS

IV

TO BEGIN AT THE BEGINNING

This book began with a poem torn out of *The New Yorker*, or *The Journal of Philanthropy*, or *Christian Century*, or *English Journal*. I had no thought of an anthology, only that I was intrigued by the voice of the poem and wanted to savor it again or to read it aloud to my students or colleagues. Mostly, the hook that snagged my attention was the voice.

Robert Frost said, "The height of poetry is in dramatic give and take. Drama is the capstone of poetry." Of course it is not exactly the voice of the poet that one hears. As T.S. Eliot explains, it is "the voice of the poet when he...create[s] a dramatic character speaking in verse, when he is saying, not what he would say in his own person, but only what he can say within the limits of an imaginary character addressing another imaginary person."

Whether the voice of the poet or of an imaginary character, in these 85 poems I hear someone I recognize—the math teacher across the hall; a colleague whose passing I mourn; a professor whose fingerprints are all over my life; a student who, I recognize, will do what I cannot; a classmate remembered over decades, who said what I was thinking; a joke or a jest like an arrow.

This accounts for the order in which you will encounter poems in this book. They are not organized in usual ways—alphabetically by author, chronologically, or by subject. In the four sections you will hear something like threads of four conversations, voices responding to one another; objecting, rebutting, reflecting.

The first voice saved in my desk drawer might have been John Ciardi's in "On Flunking a Nice Boy Out of School." I recognized the throw-down-your-red-pencil exasperation behind "It's three months work I want" and not these "martyred repentances from you!"

Or the first in the manila folder might have been Andrew Hudgins's "The Benedictine Hand," the vivid tribute to his biology teacher. Mrs. Claw, demonstrating how not to push the glass tube through the stopper "...drove the jagged end of glass into her palm" and "with what steel/ you held before us your new deformity,/ named it, and blessed us with your error."

Certainly one of the first three filed was "Zimmer's Head Thudding Against the Blackboard"—Paul Zimmer's perfect revenge on "the old exasperated nun" who "Began to pound my head against /My six mistakes."

Jim Sutton's *"Lingua Latina & Al."* came from *Phi Delta Kappan*. Brian Doyle's "Poem for a Son Going off to College" I ripped out of *Christian Century*. I first heard Joyce Carol Oates's voice in "Nostalgia (Rural District School #7, New York)" in 1998 in *The New Yorker*.

Other voices stopped me still over the years: Taylor Mali's in "What Teachers Make." Preach it, brother! And Lou Lipstiz's shouted, "The hell with universities," standing with "WGF Who Was Told He Didn't Publish Enough to be Promoted to Associate Professor." Other poems call to mind memorable and beloved teachers.

Reading Theodore Roethke's "Elegy for Jane, My Student Thrown by a Horse" always calls up Lyall Powers, professor of practical criticism at University of Michigan, reading the closing lines, "I with no rights in the matter,/ Neither father nor lover."

Reading The Prologue to *The Canterbury Tales*, I hear over the decades the voice of my Calvin College English professor John Timmerman and recall his delight in Middle English and in Chaucer's characters. Dr. Timmerman stands beside the Clerk of Oxenford, the medieval scholar who had "Twenty bookes clad in blak and reed." Like generations of teachers I aspire to Chaucer's summary of the clerk for my epitaph: "Gladly would he lerne and gladly teche."

In re-publishing these poems I mean to lift a glass and raise a toast to the teachers and mentors I have respected, admired, and loved; to colleagues over these 50 years, some of them heroes in the pantheon of great teacher-scholars. Many of these are now among St. Paul's "great crowd of witnesses" rank on rank in the heavenly stadium but still cheering on the rest of us. And I salute my students, especially you who tolerated my foibles and inspired me to better teaching.

Here's to the schools that shaped us, for better and for worse: St. Peter Claver, Rural District School #7, North San Juan School, Rhodes Junior School and thousands of others across the land. Schools we remember with nostalgia or regret, staffed by petty tyrants, saints, and some of the wisest and most wonderful human beings, of whom the world is not worthy. For some of those teachers and professors we were forgotten at the end of the term, just a line in a grade book; for others, each of us was a work of art from the studio of the Great Artist, of eternal value, gems to be set in silver or gold.

My first grade teacher was Marianne Vander Griend. A lady, married in middle age, she loved me. She was from South Africa and had a strong accent. I can still hear her pronounce my name. My very last teacher was Albert Marckwardt, a scholar, a philologist retired from Princeton and then invited back to Ann Arbor. Professor Marckwardt taught a 700-level course in the history of the English language, and guided my directed study to shape a dissertation. A great man of the old school, he had not heard about grade inflation and would not have been interested anyway. Between these two bookends, Mrs. Vander Griend and Professor Marckwardt, were about one hundred instructors, teachers, professors, coaches, and mentors. Most were decent, reasonably competent professionals. This book thanks the truly memorable people who changed me for the better by word and example. What distinguishes the great ones is that they taught me and my schoolmates. Certainly they taught math or geography or Latin or English — but their focus was their students.

Here's to the adults there who held up the roof of our world and to our classmates, long gone, who still populate it. Garrison Keillor writes that "The living wander away, we don't hear from them for months, years — but the dead move in with us to stay. They exhort us to greater faithfulness, forgive us our inertia, comfort us in our agitation." We remember you, Timothy Winters, Sietse Buning,

Ruth, and Christian—and the thousand friends in a receding line behind them. Here's to the boy who, considered a bit odd, played with paper dolls on the front steps of grammar school; and to my good friend who never ran out at recess to play kick ball, or soccer, or dog & deer, or keepaway. What was he doing? I wonder now. Here's to Bill, who raised his hand just once in 4th grade. When the teacher asked, "What did Magellan's men do after he was killed?" Bill offered: "They buried him?" I remember you, Dixon, at 10 a little dictator. "Everybody who wants to be on my team, come over here." You taught me to stand with underdogs. Here's to Harlan for kicking the soccer ball over the road and down the bank to the slough just as the bell rang—so he and I had a legitimate excuse for being tardy.

Here's to classmates and friends who influenced us more than any college course. To Dennis, who recited with a glint in his eye, "I cheer a dead man's sweetheart—never ask me whose." To my shipmate Karl, standing the mid-watch with me in the South China Sea. On the wing of the bridge, the ship slowly rolling. Karl argued for the power of rhyme and proved his point by reciting into the dark night Housman's "Loveliest of Trees, the Cherry Now" and "To an Athlete Dying Young." To Joanne, who defended Wallace Stevens over T.S. Eliot; showed me how *The Portrait of a Lady* is the great American novel; and convinced me that Joyce Carol Oates is a serious major writer.

Finally, I intend this book as a gift, a very modest memento, to all my colleagues in schools and colleges and universities who chose a life of significance, a life that made a difference—the teaching life.

To name just one "dean of faculty," one team captain from each school I served: John Warners, Michael Wolfe, Lillian Eiten, Ray Vanderlaan, Karen Elliot, and Andrew Kleyn. Behind each of these is a long line of wise, competent, passionate, large-hearted, tenacious, and brave teachers I am proud to stand with.

In his Nobel Prize acceptance speech, at an ominous time in the Cold War, William Faulkner addressed writers, and by extension teachers. At a time when "the only question was: When will I be blown up?" Faulkner said, "man will not only endure, he will prevail." This is a good time to remind each other what Faulkner said about writers and, I believe, about teachers. Man will prevail "because he has a soul, a spirit capable of compassion and sacrifice and endurance. The poet's…duty is to write about these things. It is his privilege to help man endure by lifting his heart, by reminding him of the courage and honor and hope and pride and compassion and pity and sacrifice which have been the glory of his past." I am proud of colleagues for caring deeply about, teaching, and inspiring their students to those "old verities and truths of the heart."

You inspired me, friends, and made me better than myself. I am proud to stand with you in the noble fraternity of educators. With you I would climb Everest, carry the ring to Mordor, charge the beach at Normandy. With you, comrades, I'd do it all over again.

—*J. Barry Koops*

I

THE BENEDICTINE HAND

"Now, class," she said, "we must be careful when
we push the glass tube through the stopper, thus."
She slid it halfway through the rubber hole.
It stuck. She rammed it harder, twisted. It snapped,
and snapping, drove the jagged end of glass
into her palm. Blood dribbled on the desk.

"Now that's what you are not supposed to do,"
she said. She held two frozen fingers up,
as if to bless us. "I've cut the median nerve.
This is what's called the Benedictine Hand.
It's paralyzed." She flexed her thumb and last
two fingers. The blessing fingers stayed erect.
Then, pale, she wrapped her red hand in a wad
of towels, left the room—quick, angry steps.

We boys, although it wasn't accurate,
thereafter called her Mrs. Claw, not telling
each other how we wept that night or how,
dear Mrs. Claw, we won't forget the bright
blood, Benedictine Hand, or with what steel
you held before us your new deformity,
named it, explained it, and blessed us with your error.

—Andrew Hudgins

WHAT MY TEACHERS TAUGHT ME
I TRY TO TEACH MY STUDENTS

A bird in the hand
is not to be desired.
In writing, nothing
is too much trouble.
Culture is nourished, not
by fact, but by myth.
Continually think of those
who were truly great
who in their lives fought
for life, who wore
at their hearts, the fire's
center. Feel the meanings
the words hide. Make routine
a stimulus. Remember
it can cease. Forge
hosannahs from doubt.
Hammer on doors with the heart.
All occasions invite God's
mercies and all times
are his seasons.

—Maura Eichner

SEPTEMBER, THE FIRST DAY OF SCHOOL

I

My child and I hold hands on the way to school,
And when I leave him at the first-grade door
He cries a little but is brave; he does
Let go. My selfish tears remind me how
I cried before that door a life ago.
I may have had a hard time letting go.

Each fall the children must endure together
What every child also endures alone:
Learning the alphabet, the integers,
Three dozen bits and pieces of a stuff
So arbitrary, so peremptory,
That worlds invisible and visible

Bow down before it, as in Joseph's dream
The sheaves bowed down and then the stars bowed down
Before the dreaming of a little boy.
That dream got him such hatred of his brothers
As cost the greater part of life to mend,
And yet great kindness came of it in the end.

II

A school is where they grind the grain of thought,
And grind the children who must mind the thought.
It may be those two grindings are but one,
As from the alphabet come Shakespeare's plays,
As from the integers comes Euler's Law,
As from the whole, inseparably, the lives,

The shrunken lives that have not been set free
By law or by poetic phantasy.
But may they be. My child has disappeared
Behind the schoolroom door. And should I live
To see his coming forth, a life away,
I know my hope, but do not know its form

Nor hope to know it. May the fathers he finds
Among his teachers have a care of him
More than his father could. How that will look
I do not know, I do not need to know.
Even our tears belong to ritual.
But may great kindness come of it in the end.

—Howard Nemerov

September 12

CLEAR AND SUNNY

I heard it again this morning—
the music of the playground.
Worried that I would not hear it,
I had listened as soon as I left the house,
and there it was,
softened by all the green leaves in the tall trees,
rich like thick jam on buttered bread,
more beautiful than church bells:
the shouts and laughter of schoolchildren,
bubbling through air waves still trembling
with the terrible news of
yesterday.

—David Schelhaas

THE SCHOOL CHILDREN

The children go forward with their little satchels.
And all morning the mothers have labored
to gather the late apples, red and gold,
like words of another language.

And on the other shore
are those who wait behind great desks
to receive these offerings.

How orderly they are—the nails
on which the children hang
their overcoats of blue or yellow wool.

And the teachers shall instruct them in silence
and the mothers shall scour the orchards for a way out,
drawing to themselves the gray limbs of the fruit trees
bearing so little ammunition.

—Louise Glück

DOLOR

I have known the inexorable sadness of pencils,
Neat in their boxes, dolor of pad and paper-weight,
All the misery of manila folders and mucilage,
Desolation in immaculate public places,
Lonely reception room, lavatory, switchboard,
The unalterable pathos of basin and pitcher,
Ritual of multigraph, paper-clip, comma,
Endless duplication of lives and objects.
And I have seen dust from the walls of institutions,
Finer than flour, alive, more dangerous than silica,
Sift, almost invisible, through long afternoons of tedium,
Dropping a fine film on nails and delicate eyebrows,
Glazing the pale hair, the duplicate gray standard faces.

— Theodore Roethke

LANGUAGE LESSONS

The carpet in the kindergarten room
was alphabet blocks; all of us fidgeting
on bright, primary letters. On the shelf
sat that week's inflatable sound. The *th*
was shaped like a tooth. We sang
about brushing up and down, practiced
exhaling while touching our tongues
to our teeth. Next week, a puffy U
like an upside-down umbrella; the rest
of the alphabet deflated. Some days,
we saw parents through the windows
to the hallway sky. *Look, a fat lady*,
a boy beside me giggled. Until then
I'd only known my mother as beautiful.

—Alexandra Teague

FIRST GRADE

Until then, every forest
had wolves in it, we thought
it would be fun to wear snowshoes
all the time, and we could talk to water.

So who is this woman with the gray
breath calling out names and pointing
to the little desks we will occupy
for the rest of our lives?

—Ron Koertge

LEARNING IN THE FIRST GRADE

"The cup is red. The drop of rain
is blue. The clam is brown."

So said the sheet of exercises–
purple mimeos, still heady
from the fluid in the rolling
silver drum. But the cup was

not red. It was white,
or had no color of its own.

Oh, but my mind was finical.
It put the teacher perpetually
in the wrong. Called on, however,
I said aloud: "The cup is red."

"But it's not," I thought,
like Galileo Galilei
muttering under his beard....

—Jane Kenyon

TROUBLE WITH MATH IN A ONE-ROOM COUNTRY SCHOOL

The others bent their heads and started in.
Confused, I asked my neighbor
to explain—a sturdy, bright-cheeked girl
who brought raw milk to school from her family's
herd of Holsteins. Ann had a blue bookmark,
and on it Christ revealed his beating heart,
holding the flesh back with His wounded hand.
Ann understood division....

Miss Moran sprang from her monumental desk
and led me roughly through the class
without a word. My shame was radical
as she propelled me past the cloakroom
to the furnace closet, where only the boys
were put, only the older ones at that.
The door swung briskly shut.

The warmth, the gloom, the smell
of sweeping compound clinging to the broom
soothed me. I found a bucket, turned it
upside down, and sat, hugging my knees.
I hummed a theme from Haydn that I knew
from my piano lessons....
and hardened my heart against authority.
And then I heard her steps, her fingers
on the latch. She led me, blinking
and changed, back to the class.

—Jane Kenyon

MRS. KRIKORIAN

She saved me. When I arrived in 6th grade,
a known criminal, the new teacher
asked me to stay after school the first day, she said
I've heard about you. She was a tall woman,
with a deep crevice between her breasts,
and a large, calm nose. She said,
This is a special library pass.
As soon as you finish your hour's work—
that hour's work that took ten minutes
and then the devil glanced into the room
and found me empty, a house standing open—
you can go to the library. Every hour
I'd zip through the work in a dash and slip out of my
seat as if out of God's side and sail
down to the library, solo through the empty
powerful halls, flash my pass
and stroll over to the dictionary
to look up the most interesting word
I knew, *spank*, dipping two fingers
into the jar of library paste to
suck that tart mucilage as I
came to the page with the cocker spaniel's
silks curling up like the fine steam of the body.
After *spank*, and *breast*, I'd move on
to *Abe Lincoln* and *Helen Keller*,
safe in their goodness till the bell, thanks
to Mrs. Krikorian, amiable giantess
with the kind eyes. When she asked me to write
a play, and direct it, and it was a flop, and I

hid in the coat-closet, she brought me a candy-cane
as you lay a peppermint on the tongue, and the worm
will come up out of the bowel to get it.
And so I was emptied of Lucifer
and filled with school glue and eros and
Amelia Earhart, saved by Mrs. Krikorian.
And who had saved Mrs. Krikorian?
When the Turks came across Armenia, who
slid her into the belly of a quilt, who
locked her in a chest, who mailed her to America?
And *that* one, who saved *her*, and *that* one—
who saved *her*, to save the one
who saved Mrs. Krikorian, who was
standing there on the sill of 6th grade, a
wide-hipped angel, smokey hair
standing up weightless all around her head?
I end up owing my soul to so many,
to the Armenian nation, one more soul someone
jammed behind a stove, drove
deep into a crack in a wall,
shoved under a bed. I would wake
up, in the morning, under my bed—not
knowing how I had got there—and lie
in the dusk, the dustballs beside my face
round and ashen, shining slightly
with the eerie comfort of what is neither good nor evil.

—*Sharon Olds*

THE SECRET

Two girls discover
the secret of life
in a sudden line of
poetry.

I who don't know the
secret wrote
the line. They
told me

(through a third person)
they had found it
but not what it was,
not even

what line it was. No doubt
by now, more than a week
later, they have forgotten
the secret,

the line, the name of
the poem. I love them
for finding what
I can't find,

and for loving me
for the line I wrote,
and for forgetting it
so that

a thousand times, till death
finds them, they may
discover it again, in other
lines

in other
happenings. And for
wanting to know it,
for

assuming there is
such a secret, yes,
for that
most of all.

—Denise Levertov

AMONG CHILDREN

I walk among the rows of bowed heads—
the children are sleeping through fourth grade
so as to be ready for what is ahead,
the monumental boredom of junior high
and the rush forward tearing their wings
loose and turning their eyes forever inward.
These are the children of Flint, their fathers
work at the spark plug factory or truck
bottled water in 5 gallon sea-blue jugs
to the widows of the suburbs. You can see
already how their backs have thickened,
how their small hands, soiled by pig iron,
leap and stutter even in dreams. I would like
to sit down among them and read slowly
from *The Book of Job* until the windows
pale and the teacher rises out of a milky sea
of industrial scum, her gowns streaming
with light, her foolish words transformed
into song, I would like to arm each one
with a quiver of arrows so that they might
rush like wind there where no battle rages
shouting among the trumpets, Ha! Ha!
How dear the gift of laughter in the face
of the 8 hour day, the cold winter mornings
without coffee and oranges, the long lines
of mothers in old coats waiting silently
where the gates have closed. Ten years ago
I went among these same children, just born,
in the bright ward of the Sacred Heart and leaned

down to hear their breaths delivered that day,
burning with joy. There was such wonder
in their sleep, such purpose in their eyes
closed against autumn, in their damp heads
blurred with the hair of ponds, and not one
turned against me or the light, not one
said, I am sick, I am tired, I will go home,
not one complained or drifted alone,
unloved, on the hardest day of their lives.
Eleven years from now they will become
the men and women of Flint or Paradise,
the majors of a minor town, and I
will be gone into smoke or memory,
so I bow to them here and whisper
all I know, all I will never know.

—Philip Levine

THE GEOGRAPHY OF CHILDREN

"I remember having seen somewhere a geography text which began thus: 'What is the world? It is a cardboard globe.' Such precisely is the geography of children." —*Jean-Jacques Rousseau, from* Emile

Geography is the room at the top of the stairs
where Mr. Haugh reigns, waving a yardstick —
first stop on the rise to seventh grade.
He sizes us up with bulging eyes, rattles
his keychain. Already he knows, and so do we,
who'll make trouble, which girls he'll tease,
which boy will taste his simmering rage.

Flexing his gauge, he begins the long slog
over a cardboard sea, holding up for us
strange creatures who eat dogs or scar
themselves or stalk their prey with poisoned darts.
Meanwhile Carl Rudy perfects the art
 of rolling his eyes back in his head like Caesar.
Carolyn Adams and Susie Breidenthal
agree they won't walk to school with me anymore.

"This is the Amazon," says Mr. Haugh.
We chew paper, toy with the rubber bands
on our new braces, till they pop or fly off
like tropical bees. He crosses the equator
and stalks north along the seventy-eighth
meridian. We study each other's necks and knees,
the clock, the cracks, the scratches on our desks
which truly, truly show us the way.

—Jane Flanders

SNOW DAY

Today we woke up to a revolution of snow,
its white flag waving over everything,
the landscape vanished,
not a single mouse to punctuate the blankness,
and beyond these windows

the government buildings smothered,
schools and libraries buried, the post office lost
under the noiseless drift,
the paths of trains softly blocked,
the world fallen under this falling.

In a while, I will put on some boots
and step out like someone walking in water,
and the dog will porpoise through the drifts,
and I will shake a laden branch
sending a cold shower down on us both.

But for now I am a willing prisoner in this house,
a sympathizer with the anarchic cause of snow.
I will make a pot of tea
and listen to the plastic radio on the counter,
as glad as anyone to hear the news

that the Kiddie Corner School is closed,
the Ding-Dong School, closed.
The All Aboard Children's School, closed,
the Hi-Ho Nursery School, closed,
along with—some will be delighted to hear—

the Toadstool School, the Little School,
Little Sparrows Nursery School,
Little Stars Pre-School, Peas-and-Carrots Day School,
the Tom Thumb Child Center, all closed
and — clap your hands — the Peanuts Play School.

So this is where the children hide all day,
These are the nests where they letter and draw,
where they put on their bright miniature jackets,
all darting and climbing and sliding,
all but the few girls whispering by the fence.

And now I am listening hard
in the grandiose silence of the snow,
trying to hear what those three girls are plotting,
what riot is afoot,
which small queen is about to be brought down.

—*Billy Collins*

THE SACRED

After the teacher asked if anyone had
      a sacred place
and the students fidgeted and shrank

in their chairs, the most serious of them all
      said it was his car,
being in it alone, his tape deck playing

things he'd chosen, and others knew the truth
      had been spoken
and began speaking about their rooms,

their hiding places, but the car kept coming
      up, the car in motion,
music filling it, and sometimes one other person

who understood the bright altar of the dashboard
      and how far away
a car could take him from the need

to speak, or to answer, the key
      in having a key
and putting it in, and going.

—Stephen Dunn

SECONDARY ED

For Jack Kuipers

In high school no teacher told us
that algebra's abstract equations
glue together a near-infinity
of molecules and tractors and stars,
or that geometry lays out
the shape and essence
of the mind's argument with itself.
No one said how the cadences
and leaps of the human heart
imprint themselves on an underlay
the Greeks measured and called iambic.

Failing to stay the set courses,
I listened out of school
to nickel junk-shop recordings
by the Hot Five Jelly Roll & Bix,
found the scale of things,
how separate arcs relate, heard
some counterpoint, caught a sense
of lines that crystallize into shapes
formed by the pressures inside them.

Such wild hot math helped me
sneak into college without a diploma
and cut me wide open to Plato &
Shakespeare, then Homer, Keats.
Still—why does stirred water
form bubbles that are perfect spheres?
And how does anyone understand
the mysterious presence of *pi*?

—Rod Jellema

EXECUTION

The last time I saw my high school football coach
He had cancer stenciled into his face
Like pencil marks from the sun, like intricate
Drawings on the chalkboard, small *x's* and *o's*
That he copied down in a neat numerical hand
Before practice in the morning. By day's end
The board was a spiderweb of options and counters,
Blasts and sweeps, a constellation of players
Shining under his favorite word, *Execution*,
Underlined in the upper right-hand corner of things.
He believed in football like a new religion
And had perfect, unquestioning faith in the fundamentals
Of blocking and tackling, the idea of warfare
Without suffering or death, the concept of teammates
Moving in harmony like the planets — and yet
Our awkward adolescent bodies were always canceling
The flawless beauty of Saturday afternoons in September,
Falling away from the particular grace of autumn,
The clear weather, the ideal game he imagined.
And so he drove us through punishing drills
On weekday afternoons, and doubled our practice time,
And challenged us to hammer him with forearms,
And devised elaborate, last-second plays — a flea-
Flicker, a triple reverse — to save us from defeat.

Almost always they worked. He despised losing
And loved winning more than his own body, maybe even
More than himself. But the last time I saw him
He looked wobbly and stunned by illness,
And I remembered the game in my senior year
When we met a downstate team who loved hitting
More than we did, who battered us all afternoon
With a vengeance, who destroyed us with timing
And power, with deadly, impersonal authority,
Machine-like fury, perfect execution.

—*Edward Hirsch*

HOW THEY PLAY

For John Moore

There are times on the floor
when they do what the book says
and the coaches have hammered home.
Hands are up on "D"
and the switches are working.
You see nervousness
in the squeaking shuffle of feet,
worry and peevishness
in the walk back
to the huddle. But then

when the game is on
and the visitors are shooting
lights out
there comes a moment
when the Spirit
had better come
and somebody'd
better fly
through the needle's
eye, or else. And somebody

does. Undesirable
possible futures
flake away and on the rebound
of a rebound
of a rebound

grace appears, in
high top shoes,
and through a forest
of limbs hangs one

on the rim
before
it drops and writes
the script.

We will look back
on that moment
as the best in
that day and look
ahead
at other moments, other
games
and wonder
how grace might
ever again
appear

round and orange
through a forest of limbs.

—Randall VanderMey

AT THE CHORAL CONCERT

The high school kids are so beautiful
in their lavender blouses and crisp white shirts.

They open their mouths to sing with that
far-off stare they had looking out from the crib.

Their voices lift up from the marble bed
of the high altar to the blue endless ceiling

of heaven as depicted in the cloudy dome —
and we — as the parents — crane our necks

to see our children and what is above us —
and ahead of us — until the end when we

are invited up to sing with them — sopranos
and altos — tenors and basses — to sing the great

Hallelujah Chorus — and I'm standing with the other
stunned and gray fathers — holding our sheet music —

searching for our parts — and we realize —
our voices are surprisingly rich — experienced —

For the Lord God omnipotent reigneth —
and how do we all know to come in

at exactly the right moment?—*Forever and ever*—
and how can it not seem that we shall reign

forever and ever—in one voice with our beautiful
children—looking out into all those lights.

—Tim Nolan

SCHOOLGIRLS ROWING

Five twelve-year-olds in short white skirts,
skinny, long-legged, filling out
but chattering with treble voices still,
are teetering over the edge of adolescence
and the slender yellow boat.
'Sir!' says blonde bunches, 'What are we 'sposed to do?
There's water up to the clogs. It's practically full!'
'It's disgusting, Sir,' adds brown plaits,
'How are we 'sposed to row?'
'Shut up, girls,' the coach says, 'and get out.'
The *Dickie Richards*, with due fuss, is turned and drained.
Smiling now, back in, they push off well.
'Square your blade, Four,' says the cox,
'I keep telling you, Danielle!'
Coincidence or foul play from Prince's passing by
sends duck-weed and a snigger or two their way.
'Don't buck your oar, Jane,' calls the coach.
'Kim, you're taking too much reach,
and watch that feathering height!'
As Saint's, ship-shape in white and gold,
draw level in the *Piping Shrike*,
their number three looks sideways, washing out;
they steer right through the weed.

The girls stay straight-faced, lift their chins
and pull more smoothly with each stroke;
sleekly the *Dickie Richards* cuts the murky green.
Past the boys and under the bridge
skim Alison, Danielle, Rebecca, Kim and Jane;
the ripples in their wake
touch *Popeye* at the river's edge
with alpha waves of light.
You're on the bank, just sitting in the sun,
but suddenly happiness has you by the throat.

—Jan Owen

POEM FOR A SON GOING OFF TO COLLEGE

Looking at photographs of the kids. One of them is going
To college tomorrow. I used to wear that kid like a jacket.
He fell asleep instantly given the slightest chance. School,
The car, even once during a time-out at a basketball game,
Although to be fair he was the point guard and had played
The whole first half and been double-teamed. He could be
Laughing at something and you'd turn away to see a hawk
Or his lissome mom and when you turned back he was *out*.
But tomorrow he's in the top bunk in a room far away. We
Will leave the back porch light on for him out of habit and
In the morning we will both notice that it's still on and one
Of us will cry right into the coffee beans and the other will
Remember that it felt like all the poems we mean when we
Say words like *dad* and *son* and *love* when I slung that boy
Over one shoulder or another or carried him amidships like
A sack of rice or best of all dangling him by his feet so that
All the nickels he put in his pockets for just this eventuality
Poured down like something else we do not have words for.

—Brian Doyle

II

ONE ROOM

The one-room school
sitting for its photograph
could have been my students
and the faces
are not happy June ones—
one girl worried
about her dark dress
amidst the light frilly ones,
two boys uncomfortable in jackets,
the rest scolded solemn
as if the teacher were taking
mug shots.
I know that the lad on the left
who climbed the schoolyard pine
and threw down the hawk's eggs,
bombing the future,
died later by drowning,
dumped from his canoe.
I wonder if the girl in the middle,
blessed with alcoholic parents,
now buys overshoes compulsively
so her child will never wear
plastic sandals in January.
And I still see the ones
who brought garter snakes,
carried water for the drinking urn
and pounded blackboard erasers
bending over me

after the baseball knocked me down
at recess and asking me if I'm okay.
I am, and long
to ask them the same.

—Diane Dawber

TIMOTHY WINTERS

Timothy Winters comes to school
With eyes as wide as a football-pool,
Ears like bombs and teeth like splinters:
A blitz of a boy is Timothy Winters.

His belly is white, his neck is dark,
And his hair is an exclamation-mark.
His clothes are enough to scare a crow
And through his britches the blue winds blow.

When teacher talks he won't hear a word
And he shoots down dead the arithmetic-bird,
He licks the patterns off his plate
And he's not even heard of the Welfare State.

Timothy Winters has bloody feet
And he lives in a house on Suez Street,
He sleeps in a sack on the kitchen floor
And they say there aren't boys like him any more.

Old Man Winters likes his beer
And his missus ran off with a bombardier,
Grandma sits in the grate with a gin
And Timothy's dosed with an aspirin.

The Welfare Worker lies awake
But the law's as tricky as a ten-foot snake,
So Timothy Winters drinks his cup
And slowly goes on growing up.

At Morning Prayers the Master helves
For children less fortunate than ourselves,
And the loudest response in the room is when
Timothy Winters roars "Amen!"
So come one angel, come on ten:

Timothy Winters says "Amen
Amen amen amen amen."
Timothy Winters, Lord.
                        Amen.

                                —Charles Causley

POEM FOR CHRISTIAN, MY STUDENT

He reminds me of someone I used to know,
but who? Before class,
he comes to my office to shmooze,
a thousand thousand pointless interesting
speculations. Irrepressible boy,
his assignments are rarely completed,
or actually started. This week, instead
of research in the stacks, he's performing
with a reggae band that didn't exist last week.
Kids danced to his music
and stripped, he tells me gleefully,
high spirit of the street festival.
He's the singer, of course—
why ask if he studied an instrument?
On the brink of graduating with
an engineering degree (not, it turned out,
his forte), he switched to English,
his second language. It's hard to swallow
the bravura of his academic escapes
or tell if the dark eyes laugh with his face.
Once, he brought me a tiny persimmon
he'd picked on campus; once, a poem
about an elderly friend in New Delhi
who left him volumes of Tagore
and memories of avuncular conversation.
My encouragement makes him skittish—
it doesn't suit his jubilant histrionics
of despair. And I remember myself
shrinking from enthusiasm or praise,

the prospect of effort-drudgery.
Success—a threat. A future, we figure,
of revision—yet what can the future be
but revision and repair? Now, on the brink
again, graduation's postponed, the brilliant
thesis on Walker Percy unwritten.
"I'll drive to New Orleans and soak
it up and write my paper in a weekend,"
he announces in the Honors office.
And, "I want to be a bum in daytime
and a reggae star at night!"
What could I give him from my life
or art that matters, how share
the desperate slumber of my early years,
the flashes of inspiration and passion
in a life on hold? If I didn't fool
myself or anyone, no one could touch
me, or tell me much … This gloomy
Houston Monday, he appears at my door,
so sunny I wouldn't dare to wake him
now, or say it matters if he wakes at all.
"Write a poem about me!" he commands,
and so I do.

—Gail Mazur

STUDENT

The green shell of his backpack makes him lean
into wave after wave of responsibility,
and he swings his stiff arms and cupped hands,

paddling ahead. He has extended his neck
to its full length, and his chin, hard as a beak,
breaks the cold surf. He's got his baseball cap on

backward as he crawls out of the froth
of a hangover and onto the sand of the future,
and lumbers, heavy with hope, into the library.

— Ted Kooser

AT THE PLAYGROUND

Away down deep and away up high,
a swing drops you into the sky.
Back it draws you away down deep,
forth it flings you in a sweep
all the way to the stars and back
— Goodbye, Jill; Goodbye, Jack;
shuddering climb wild and steep,
away up high, away down deep.

— William Stafford

HULL HUMANITY

"Hey, here's your sandwich," I called across the lunchroom
to Caldwell, the kid we picked on.
He was fat and unathletic,
and we kept him in his place.

Right in style,
I threw the sandwich I had swiped from him. He reached,
missed,
and the waxed paper burst apart
against the lunchroom window.
A smear of mayonnaise streaked the glass,
a flap of bologna hung over the back of a desk,
a lettuce leaf and a tomato slice lay on the floor.
I smiled triumphantly,
the boys' lunchroom laughed adoringly,
and then we heard Mr. Leonard's voice.
He had stepped in without our noticing.

> "Caldwell,
> here is my sandwich.
> Enjoy it.
> Sietze,
> may I see you out in the hall?"

> > "OH oh."
> > "Naughty Sietze."
> > "Now you'll catch it."
> > I was afraid.

In the hall
Mr. Leonard said quietly,
"People throw food only at animals."

"Yes, Mr. Leonard," I said.
He did not need to tell me to go for
mop, cloth, and soapy water.

From then on
Caldwell was different for me
and I was decent to him.

Once or twice later
I have felt as alienated as Caldwell must have then.
Depressed,
I can always find comfort
in how efficiently a waitress pours my coffee,
in how a check-out girl smiles as she makes change,
and in how you, dear, ladle me a bowl of cheese soup
      and wipe the inside of the rim
      so that the line of yellow-green soup
      will be sharp against the brown pottery,
and I remember that people throw food only to animals,
and I tell myself,
"Sietze, you're not such a dog as you think you are."

—Sietze Buning

THE SALLY ROD

On the main street of Granard I met Duffy
Whom I had known before the age of reason
In short trousers in the Senior Infants' room
Where once upon a winter's day Miss Walls
Lost her head and cut the legs off us
For dirty talk we didn't think she'd hear.
"Well, for Jesus' sake," cried Duffy, coming at me
With his stick in the air and two wide open arms,
"For Jesus' sake! D'you mind the sally rod?"

—Seamus Heaney

POEM BEGINNING WITH A LINE
MEMORIZED AT SCHOOL

Whither, indeed, *midst falling dew*,
Whither, Miss Pfisterer, black-dressed and balding
Teacher of English, lover of Bryant,
Whither did we all pursue
White glow the heavens with the last somethingsomething?

Bradley Lewis, I mean:
Who put aside with his cello and his brushes
Our lusty masculine sneers at his graceful ways,
Skipped the civics exam to father a son
And now designs engines with Mozart turned up loud.

Kenny Kruiter, I mean:
Expelled from high school for incantation with wine,
Who bends the knee to his common daily bread,
Hacks every day at bleeding sides of beef
And cheers twice a week the college basketball team.

Michael Slochak, I mean:
He always stuttered every dull thing he knew
And walked home alone—past home, to one gold period
When, crimson phrase against the darkly sky,
His jet purred into a green Korean hill.

—Rod Jellema

FIRST LOVE

Titian's Young Englishman with a Glove, *circa 1530*

It happened in Physics,
reading a Library art book under the desk,
(the lesson was Archimedes in the bath)
I turned a page and fell
for an older man, and anonymous at that,
hardly ideal—
he was four hundred and forty five,
I was fourteen.
"Eureka!" streaked each thought
(I prayed no-one would hear)
and Paradise all term
was page 179
(I prayed no-one would guess).
Of course
my fingers, sticky with toffee and bliss,
failed to entice him from his century;
his cool grey stare
fastened me firmly in mine.
I got six overdues,
suspension of borrowing rights
and a D in Physics
but had by heart what Archimedes proves.
Ten years later I married:
a European with cool grey eyes,
a moustache,
pigskin gloves.

—Jan Owen

THE PICNIC

It is the picnic with Ruth in the spring.
Ruth was third on my list of seven girls
But the first two were gone (Betty) or else
Had someone (Ellen has accepted Doug).
Indian Gully the last day of school;
Girls make the lunches for the boys too.
I wrote a note to Ruth in algebra class
Day before the test. She smiled, and nodded.
We left the cars and walked through the young corn
The shoots green as paint and the leaves like tongues
Trembling. Beyond the fence where we stood
Some wild strawberry flowered by an elm tree
And Jack-in-the-pulpit was olive ripe.
A blackbird fled as I crossed, and showed
A spot of gold or red under its quick wing.
I held the wire for Ruth and watched the whip
Of her long, striped skirt as she followed.
Three freckles blossomed on her thin, white back
Underneath the loop where the blouse buttoned.
We went for our lunch away from the rest,
Stretched in the new grass, our heads close
Over unknown things wrapped up in wax papers.
Ruth tried for the same, I forget what it was,
And our hands were together. She laughed,
And a breeze caught the edge of her little
Collar and the edge of her brown, loose hair
That touched my cheek. I turned my face in-
to the gentle fall. I saw how sweet it smelled.
She didn't move her head or take her hand.

I felt a soft caving in my stomach
As at the top of the highest slide
When I had been a child, but was not afraid,
And did not know why my eyes moved with wet
As I brushed her cheek with my lips and brushed
Her lips with my own lips. She said to me
Jack, Jack, different than I had ever heard,
Because she wasn't calling me, I think,
Or telling me. She used my name to
Talk in another way I wanted to know.
She laughed again and then she took her hand;
I gave her what we both had touched — can't
Remember what it was, and we ate the lunch.
Afterward we walked in the small, cool creek
Our shoes off, her skirt hitched, and she smiling,
My pants rolled, and then we climbed up the high
Side of Indian Gully and looked
Where we had been, or hands together again.
It was then some bright thing came in my eyes,
Starting at the back of them and flowing
Suddenly through my head and down my arms
And stomach and my bare legs that seemed not
To stop in feet, not to feel the red earth
Of the Gully, as though we hung in a
Touch of birds. There was a word in my throat
With the feeling and I knew the first time
What it meant and I said, it's beautiful.
Yes, she said, and I felt the sound and word
In my hand join the sound and word in hers

As in one name said, or in one cupped hand.
We put back on our shoes and socks and we
Sat in the grass awhile, crosslegged, under
A blowing tree, not saying anything.
And Ruth played with shells she found in the creek,
As I watched. Her small wrist which was so sweet
To me turned by her breast and the shells dropped
Green, white, blue, easily into her lap,
Passing light through themselves. She gave the pale
Shells to me, and got up and touched her hips
With her light hands, and we walked down slowly
To play the school games with the others.

—John Logan

ELEGY FOR JANE

My Student, Thrown by a Horse

I remember the neckcurls, limp and damp as tendrils;
And her quick look, a sidelong pickerel smile;
And how, once startled into talk, the light syllables leaped for her,
And she balanced in the delight of her thought,
A wren, happy, tail into the wind,
Her song trembling the twigs and small branches.
The shade sang with her;
The leaves, their whispers turned to kissing;
And the mold sang in the bleached valleys under the rose.

Oh, when she was sad, she cast herself down into such a pure depth,
Even a father could not find her:
Scraping her cheek against straw;
Stirring the clearest water.

My sparrow, you are not here,
Waiting like a fern, making a spiny shadow.
The sides of wet stones cannot console me,
Nor the moss, wound with the last light.

If only I could nudge you from this sleep,
My maimed darling, my skittery pigeon.
Over this damp grave I speak the word of my love:
I, with no rights in this matter,
Neither father nor lover.

— *Theodore Roethke*

EMILY SPARKS

Where is my boy, my boy—
In what far part of the world?
The boy I loved best of all in the school?—
I, the teacher, the old maid, the virgin heart,
Who made them all my children.
Did I know my boy aright,
Thinking of him as spirit aflame,
Active, ever aspiring?
Oh, boy, boy, for whom I prayed and prayed
In many a watchful hour at night,
Do you remember the letter I wrote you
Of the beautiful love of Christ?
And whether you ever took it or not,
My boy, wherever you are,
Work for your soul's sake,
That all the clay of you, all the dross of you,
May yield to the fire of you,
Till the fire is nothing but light!...
Nothing but light!

—*Edgar Lee Masters*

MRS. SNOW

Busts of the great composers glimmered in niches,
Pale stars. Poor Mrs. Snow, who could forget her,
Counting the time out in that hushed falsetto?
(How early we begin to grasp what kitsch is!)
But when she loomed above us like an alp,
We little towns below could feel her shadow.
Somehow her nods of approval seemed to matter
More than the stray flakes drifting from her scalp.
Her etchings of ruins, her mass-production Mings
Were our first culture; she put us in awe of things.
And once, with her help, I composed a waltz,
Too innocent to be completely false,
Perhaps, but full of marvelous clichés.
She beamed and softened then.
                    Ah, those were the days.

—Donald Justice

LESSONS

In our little town of soot and sulfur
the Maestro was known as a gentleman
of the old school, soft-spoken, refined.
Even my mother approved, handing him
on Saturday afternoons, the money
she scrimped, that I might profit as much
in manners as in music, blatting
my horrible cornet cadenzas
into the parlor's fractured air.
How patiently he listened, what pains
he took, urging my labors toward song!
What he loved, above all, was Mozart
and the soaring voices of bel canto.
I wanted only to be Harry James,
my famous embouchure lifting
the first fat notes of "Sleepy Lagoon"
into the ballrooms and balconies of heaven.
It all came tumbling down the night
the sheriff's spotlight found the Maestro
lurking in bushes by a bedroom window—
thus ending, so it seemed, a rash
of unsolved neighborhood complaints.
Little survived his shame: lessons,
his standing in the town, the strains
of Mozart drifting from his house—
gone, and then he was gone.
It would be years before I, too,
could leave that dying town to find
my way in the world. Yet even now

I think of him and recall those hours
on Saturday afternoons when he sat
beside me and sang into my ear
measures I could not hear for myself,
and from this distance now, in praise,
I purse my lips, as he taught me, and blow
a silent triple-tongue, staccato,
into an imaginary silver mouthpiece
of a horn once held by Harry James,
filling the sunlit rooms of Memory
with the pure, incorruptible dream of music.

—Peter Everwine

NOSTALGIA

Rural District #7, Ransomville, New York

Crumbling stone steps of the old schoolhouse
Boarded-up windows   shards of winking glass
Built 1898, numerals faint in stone as shadow
Through a window, obedient rows of desks mute
Only a droning of hornets beneath the eaves,
the cries of red-winged blackbirds by the creek

How many generations of this rocky countryside grown & gone
How many memories   & all forgotten
no one to chronicle, no regret

& the schoolhouse soon to be razed   & goodbye America
The flagless pole, what relief!
I love it, the eye lifting skyward   to nothing
Never to pledge allegiance to the United States of America
        again
Never to press my flat right hand over my heart again
        as if I had one

—*Joyce Carol Oates*

LITTLE ROCK ARKANSAS 1957

Dedicated to the nine children

Clasping like bucklers to their bodies, books,
nine children move through blasts of killing looks.
Committed to this battle each child dares,
deliberately, the fusillades of jeers.
Their valor iron in their ironed clothes
they walk politely in their polished shoes
down ambushed halls to classrooms sown with mines
to learn their lesson. Obviously nine's
a carefully calculated number, odd
not even, a suave size that can be added to, discreetly, later, or culled now
should one child break not bend; or fail to bow
sufficiently his bloody head...a rule
to heed, child, be you black and going to school.

—Isabella Gardner

AND WHEN I DREAM DREAMS

when I dream dreams, I dream of YOU,
Rhodes Jr. School
and the lockers of our minds
that were always jammed stuck
or that always hung open
and would never close,
no matter how hard You tried.
we messed up the looks of the place
and wouldn't be neat and organized
and look like we were sposed to look
and lock like we were sposed
                                        to lock.

yea that's right
I dream of you
degrees later
and from both sides of the desk
my dreams take place
in your two-way halls,
HallGuards from among us,
human traffic markers, bumps on the road
between the lanes,
to say, when we were sposed to say,
where to turn left, where right.
and how to get where you were going—
("You'll never get to high school
speakin' Spanish," I was told)
[nice of them, they thought, to not report me,
breakin' state law, school law, speakin' dirty
                    (speakin' Spanish)

and our tongues couldn't lump it
and do what they were sposed to do.
So instead I reminded others
to button buttons
and tuck shirttails in.]
I never graduated to a Cafeteria Guard,
who knew how they were picked.
We thought it had something
to do
with the FBI
or maybe the Principal's office.
So we got frisked,
Boys in one line,
Girls in another,
twice every day
entering lunch and leaving
Check - no knives on the boys.
Check - no dangerous weapons on the girls.
(like mirrors,
       perfume bottles,
          deodorant bottles,
             or teased hair.)
So we wandered the halls
cool chuck style
"no se sale"
and unawares,
never knowing
other junior highs were never frisked
never knowing
what teachers said in the teachers lounge

never knowing we were (sposed to be)
the toughest junior high in town.

And the lockers of our minds
are now assigned to other minds,
carry other books,
follow other rules,
silence other tongues,
go to other schools—
Schools of Viet Nam
Schools of cheap cafe,
Schools of dropout droppings, prison pains, and cop car's
        bulleted brains.
Marcelino thought the only way
to finance college was the Air Force
(GI Bill and good pay!)
War looked easy (compared to here)
Took his chances on a college education,
Took his pay on a shot-down helicopter
in a brown-skinned Nam,
with a pledge of allegiance in his mind
he had memorized through Spanish-speaking teeth
as a Hall Guard. "clean-cut",
Now cut clean down in a hospital ward,
paralyzed below the lips,
that still speak Spanish
slowly.
Silvia thought no one had the right
to tell her what to do.
One year out of junior high, she bitterly bore
her second pregnancy,

stabbed forks onto cafe tables
and slushed coffee through the crowds
sixteen hours a day, and she was fifteen
and still fighting to say
"I HAVE A RIGHT TO BE ME!"
Esperanza with a needle in her heart, sucking will, wanting
        junkies to say,
"Hey, you're really okay."
And Lalo with a mind that could write in his sleep
growing epics from eyes that could dream
now writes only the same story over and over
until the day
that it's all
over,
as he's frisked and he's frisked and he's frisked
and they keep finding
nothing
and even when he's out
his mind is
always in
prison
like Lupe's mind
that peels potatoes
and chops repollo
and wishes its boredom was less
than the ants in the hill
and never learned to read because
the words were in English
and she
was in Spanish.
I wonder what we would do,

Rhodes Junior School,
if we had all those
emblems of you
stamped on our lives with a big red "R"
like the letter sweaters
we could never
afford
to buy.

I keep my honorary
junior school diploma
from you
right next to the B.A., M.A.,
etcetera to a Ph.D.
because it means
I graduated
from you
and when I dream dreams,
—how I wish my dreams
had graduated too.

—*Carmen Tafolla*

INDIAN BOARDING SCHOOL: THE RUNAWAYS

Home's the place we head for in our sleep.
Boxcars stumbling north in dreams
don't wait for us. We catch them on the run.
The rails, old lacerations that we love,
shoot parallel across the face and break
just under Turtle Mountains. Riding scars
you can't get lost. Home is the place they cross.

The lame guard strikes a match and makes the dark
less tolerant. We watch through cracks in boards
as the land starts rolling, rolling till it hurts
to be here, cold in regulation clothes.
We know the sheriff's waiting at midrun
to take us back. His car is dumb and warm.
The highway doesn't rock, it only hums
like a wing of long insults. The worn-down welts
of ancient punishments lead back and forth.

All runaways wear dresses, long green ones,
the color you would think shame was. We scrub
the sidewalks down because it's shameful work.
Our brushes cut the stone in watered arcs
and in the soak frail outlines shiver clear
a moment, things us kids pressed on the dark
face before it hardened, pale, remembering
delicate old injuries, the spines of names and leaves.

—Louise Erdrich

ST. PETER CLAVER

Every town with black Catholics has a St. Peter Claver's.
My first was nursery school.
Miss Maturin made us fold our towels in a regulation square
       and nap on army cots.
No mother questioned; no child sassed.
In blue pleated skirts, pants, and white shirts,
we stood in line to use the open toilets
and conserved light by walking in darkness.
Unsmiling, mostly light-skinned, we were the children of the middle
       class, preparing to take our parents' places in a world that would
       demand we fold our hands and wait.
They said it was good for us, the bowl of soup, its pasty whiteness;
I learned to swallow and distrust my senses.

On holy cards St. Peter's face is olive-toned, his hair near kinky;
I thought he was one of us who pass between the rich and poor,
       the light and dark.
Now I read he was "a Spanish Jesuit priest who labored for
       the salvation of the African Negroes and the abolition
       of the slave trade."
I was tricked again, robbed of my patron,
 and left with a debt to another white man.

— Toi Derricotte

PAINTING THE NORTH SAN JUAN SCHOOL

White paint splotches on blue head bandanas
Dusty transistor with wired-on antenna
        plays sixties rock and roll;
Little kids came with us are on teeter-totters
        tilting under shade of oak
This building good for ten years more.
The shingled bell-cupola trembles
        at every log truck rolling by—

The radio speaks:
        today it will be one hundred degrees in the valley,
—Franquette walnuts grafted on the
        local native rootstock do o.k.
        nursery stock of cherry all has fungus;
Lucky if a bare-root planting lives,

This paint thins with water.
This year the busses will run only
        on paved roads,
Somehow the children will be taught:
How to record their mother tongue
        with written signs,

Names to all the landscape of the continent
                they live on
Assigned it by the ruling people of the last
        three hundred years,
The games of numbers,
What went before, as told by those who

think they know it,

A drunken man with chestnut mustache
Stumbles off the road to ask if he can help.

Children drinking chocolate milk

Ladders resting on the shaky porch.

—Gary Snyder

III

1905

Looking out of the front page, a wild-haired,
gentle-eyed young German man stands
before a blackboard of incomprehensible equations.
Meanwhile, back in the quotidian,
Carver takes the school to the poor.

He outfits an open truck
with shelves for his jars
of canned fruit and compost,
bins for his croker sacks of seeds.
He travels roads barely discernible
on the county map,
teaching former field-slaves
how to weave ditch weeds
into pretty table place mats,
how to keep their sweet potatoes from rotting
before winter hunger sets in,
how to make preacher-pleasing
mock fried chicken
without slaughtering a laying hen.
He notes patches of wild chicory
the farmers could collect
to free themselves from their taste
for high-priced imported caffeine.

He and his student assistants bump along
shoulder to shoulder in the high cab,
a braided scale of laughter
trailing above their raised dust.

Today, Carver is explaining,
as far as he understands it,
that fellow Einstein's "Special Theory of Relativity."
He's hardly gotten to Newtonian Space
when a platoon of skinny dogs
announces the next farm.

As they pull up,
a black man and his boy straighten,
two rows of shin-high cotton apart.
With identical gestures they remove
straw hats, wipe their foreheads with their sleeves.
Their welcoming glance meets Carver's eyes
at the velocity of light.

—*Marilyn Nelson*

M. DEGAS TEACHES ART & SCIENCE AT
DURFEE INTERMEDIATE SCHOOL
Detroit 1942

He made a line on the blackboard,
one bold stroke from right to left
diagonally downward and stood back
to ask, looking as always at no one
in particular, "What have I done?"
From the back of the room Freddie
shouted, "You've broken a piece
of chalk." M. Degas did not smile.
"What have I done?" he repeated.
The most intellectual students
looked down to study their desks
except for Gertrude Bimmler, who raised
her hand before she spoke. "M. Degas,
you have created the hypotenuse
of an isosceles triangle." Degas mused.
Everyone knew that Gertrude could not
be incorrect. "It is possible,"
Louis Warshowsky added precisely,
"that you have begun to represent
the roof of a barn." I remember
that it was exactly twenty minutes
past eleven, and I thought at worst
this would go on another forty
minutes. It was early April,
the snow had all but melted on
the playgrounds, the elms and maples
bordering the cracked walks shivered

in the new winds, and I believed
that before I knew it I'd be
swaggering to the candy store
for a Milky Way. M. Degas
pursed his lips, and the room
stilled until the long hand
of the clock moved to twenty one
as though in complicity with Gertrude,
who added confidently, "You've begun
to separate the dark from the dark."
I looked back for help, but now
the trees bucked and quaked, and I
knew this could go on forever.

—*Philip Levine*

LECCIONES DE LENGUA

She is proud of her papá
because he comes
to their little grey school,
converted from army barracks,
to teach español
to Mrs. Brenda's fifth grade.
And that means they don't
have to listen to that awful
Señora Beister on TV
with her screech owl version
of "Las mañanitas" and her annoying
forefinger to the ear,
     Escuchen
and then to the lips,
       y repitan.

He teaches them to order
Coca-Cola en el restaurán–
     Señor, quisiera una Coca, por favor–
and the names of all the utensils–
     cuchara, cuchillo, tenedor.
The children look at him funny
when he picks up the knife.
Next week he will demonstrate
the bullfights he watched
in Mexico when he was muy chiquitito.
He will choose a boy to snort, stomp,
charge the red cloth
that Papá will snap

at his side as he dodges
the sharp-horned strike,
stabs invisible swords
into the boy's hide

and makes the children laugh.

—Brenda Cárdenas

TEACHING ENGLISH FROM AN
OLD COMPOSITION BOOK

My chalk is no longer than a chip of fingernail,
Chip by which I must explain this Monday
Night the verbs "to get;" "to wear," "to cut."
I'm not given much, these tired students,
Knuckle-wrapped from work as roofers,
Sour from scrubbing toilets and pedestal sinks.
I'm given this room with five windows,
A coffee machine, a piano with busted strings,
The music of how we feel as the sun falls,
Exhausted from keeping up.

                  I stand at
The blackboard. The chalk is worn to a hangnail,
Nearly gone, the dust of some educational bone.
By and by I'm Cantiflas, the comic
Busybody in front. I say, "I get the coffee."
I pick up a coffee cup and sip.
I click my heels and say, "I wear my shoes."
I bring an invisible fork to my mouth
And say, "I eat the chicken."
Suddenly the class is alive—
Each one putting on hats and shoes,
Drinking sodas and beers, cutting flowers
And steaks—a pantomime of sumptuous living.

At break I pass out cookies.
Augustine, the Guatemalan, asks in Spanish,
"Teacher, what is 'tally-ho'?"

I look at the word in the composition book.
I raise my face to the bare bulb for a blind answer.
I stutter, then say, *"Es como adelante."*
Augustine smiles, then nudges a friend
In the next desk, now smarter by one word.
After the cookies are eaten,
We move ahead to prepositions—
"Under," "over," and "between,"
Useful words when *la migra* opens the doors
Of their idling vans.
At ten to nine, I'm tired of acting,
And they're tired of their roles.
When class ends, I clap my hands of chalk dust,
And two students applaud, thinking it's a new verb.
I tell them *adelante*,
And they pick up their old books.
They smile and, in return, cry, "Tally-ho!"
As they head for the door.

—*Gary Soto*

LINGUA LATINA & AL.

There's no such thing as true proficiency
in languages of dead or modern lands.
As Dr. Johnson said, no man can be
"good in his own & in another man's."
So there's no useful purpose I can see
in learning just to learn another tongue,
unless you think tomorrow you could be
posted to distant places or be flung
to situations linguists can't be hired,
like buying beer on Ipanema Beach.
Of Latin, Greek & French, enough; I'm tired.
Rote drives me crazy, even when I teach.
> That's how I know a thing that's meant for few
> does not oblige the rest to muddle through.

—*James Hercules Sutton*

WE REAL COOL

THE POOL PLAYERS.
SEVEN AT THE GOLDEN SHOVEL.

We real cool. We
Left school. We

Lurk late. We
Strike straight. We

Sing sin. We
Thin gin. We

Jazz June. We
Die soon.

—Gwendolyn Brooks

MRS. GOTTLIEB'S COURSE IN
WORLD LITERATURE

Few of us, she announced early on,
Were likely to have a guardian spirit devoted
To guiding us to the promised path, the one that led
To our becoming the person we were meant to be.
So if the advice of our parents and teachers
Didn't seem relevant, we'd be wise to turn
To the very books we'd be reading that semester:
Great novels and plays and poems, all starring
Versions of ourselves in situations akin
To those we'd be facing sooner than we supposed.
It wasn't too early for the girls to select
For their outside reading *Anna Karenina*.
Better find out at once how choosing passion
Above all else can sometimes leave us
Hemmed in more tightly than we were before.
As for the boys, those with a yen for detective fiction
Could write their papers on *Crime and Punishment*.
Time to move beyond asking who's the culprit
And consider what makes a crime a crime
And who is the proper judge of penitence.
So many questions to be raised and answered,
So many big decisions easy to miss
When they come disguised as small ones.
And life, she insisted, had already begun for us
Without fanfare, in earnest, at school, at home.
No way to postpone the choices held out to us
On every turn of the path we were on already.
No way to be sure we'd behave like characters

We admired when they confronted a challenge
Similar to our own, though not identical.
Just raising the question, she said, would be of use,
Along with the question how lenient a book
Were we acting in. For our sake she hoped
It had room for a second chance if we failed
The first time, not room for just one,
One door soon to be shut for good.

—*Carl Dennis*

PROMPTS (FOR HIGH SCHOOL TEACHERS WHO WRITE POETRY)

Write about walking into the building
as a new teacher. Write yourself hopeful.
Write a row of empty desks. Write the face
of a student you've almost forgotten;
he's worn a Derek Jeter jersey all year.
Do not conjecture about the adults
he goes home to, or the place he calls home.
Write about how he came to you for help
each October morning his sophomore year.
Write about teaching *Othello* to him;
write *Wherein of antres vast and deserts idle,*
rough quarries, rocks and hills whose heads touch heaven.
Write about reading his obituary
five years after he graduated. Write
a poem containing the words "common"
"core," "differentiate," and "overdose."
Write the names of the ones you will never
forget: "Jenna," "Tiberious," "Heaven,"
"Megan," "Tanya," "Kingsley," "Ashley," "David."
Write Mari with "Nobody's Baby" tattooed
in cursive on her neck, spitting sixteen bars
in the backrow, as little white Mike beatboxed
"Candy Shop" and the whole class exploded.
Write about Zuly and Nely, sisters
from Guatemala, upon whom a thousand
strange new English words rained down on like hail
each period, and who wrote the story
of their long journey on *la bestia*

through Mexico, for you, in handwriting
made heavy by the *aquís* and *ayers*
ached in their knuckles, hidden by their smiles.
Write an ode to loose-leaf. Write elegies
on the nub nose of a pink eraser.
Carve your devotion from a no. 2
pencil. Write the uncounted hours you spent
fretting about the ones who cursed you out
for keeping order, who slammed classroom doors,
who screamed "you are not my father," whose pain
unraveled and broke you, whose pain you knew.
Write how all this added up to a life.

—Dante Di Stefano

AND THE TOPIC FOR TODAY IS
ENVIRONMENTALISM. . . .
Teaching "God's Grandeur"

More politically correct than divine grandeur,
it too flames out in this small Pennsylvania town
where fracking hijacks the headlines. Good reason
and good enough to bring the state students trodding
heavily into a poem piled high with God and earth,
with "responsibilities" they hear each morning
as the gas industry trucks rattle past our windows,
their tired drivers knowing nothing
of iambic pentameter or sestets but much
about food on the table, a steady job.

The freshmen, eager now,
blurt out *dilemma, paradox, instress* —
and all those other new-sounding ideas
suddenly connected to their lives,
their parents, the sonnet
they think was written last week,
even with its 19th century,
sound-packed syllables they don't get
until slowing down, thinking.

And so — after playing with light, foil, sound;
the way trade "sears," "blears," and "smears";
and how and why shoes separate us from ground —
we detour to Genesis, Cat Stevens, and a heavy metal rendition
that almost drowns out Hopkins with bass.
All this before rounding the terrain-raked bend

to solution, which is what—they are surprised to discover—
we all most want: the eloquent octet, the bright wings,
the *ah!* that opens the mind to talk,
at long last, about the holy.

—*Marjorie Maddox*

THEME FOR ENGLISH B

The instructor said,

Go home and write
a page tonight.
And let that page come out of you —
Then, it will be true.

I wonder if it's that simple?
I am twenty-two, colored, born in Winston-Salem.
I went to school there, then Durham, then here
to this college on the hill above Harlem.
I am the only colored student in my class.
The steps from the hill lead down into Harlem,
through a park, then I cross St. Nicholas,
Eighth Avenue, Seventh, and I come to the Y,
the Harlem Branch Y, where I take the elevator
up to my room, sit down, and write this page:

It's not easy to know what is true for you or me
at twenty-two, my age. But I guess I'm what
I feel and see and hear, Harlem, I hear you:
hear you, hear me — we two — you, me, talk on this page.
(I hear New York, too.) Me — who?
Well, I like to eat, sleep, drink, and be in love.
I like to work, read, learn, and understand life.
I like a pipe for a Christmas present,
or records — Bessie, bop, or Bach.
I guess being colored doesn't make me *not* like
the same things other folks like who are other races.

So will my page be colored that I write?
Being me, it will not be white.
But it will be
a part of you, instructor.
You are white —
yet a part of me, as I am a part of you.
That's American.
Sometimes perhaps you don't want to be a part of me.
Nor do I often want to be a part of you.
But we are, that's true!
As I learn from you,
I guess you learn from me —
although you're older — and white —
and somewhat more free.

This is my page for English B.

—Langston Hughes

BETWEEN THE LINES

All that prevents him from
devoting his total attention
to the baseball game
is the pile of student writing
between him and the TV,
a stack of clichés and
tired metaphors,
worn out by a thousand previous users,
and abusers,
of the language.

He sifts through the pile
looking for one which will
motivate him to continue on
to a second and a third,
and so forth,
a metaphorical rounding of the bases,
until he has reduced the pile to nothing,
and able to turn his full attention to
the Yankees and Red Sox.

Glancing above his glasses to catch the replay
of Derek Jeter rocking a line drive
off the green monster
and only getting a single,
he ponders the mysterious twist of baseball fate
that penalizes a player for hitting the ball
too hard,
like he is penalizing himself for caring

too much,
about grading these papers.

So he pores over them
with the Fenway crowd noise
as background
until he chances across a phrase
which makes him grab the remote
and click the ball game into darkness
and stare at the screen
to see the image which has leapt off
the page in front of him
far more vivid than the night-game-green
of Fenway's infield,
reverberating louder than
the crack of Derek's bat.

—Herm Card

OBITUARY

It died last Thursday
a most cruel death
from Comp Class Critics.
Now there's nothing left.

They destroyed my poem —
ripped it limb from limb —
and in the end left only
blood splattered skin.

They said, "Your rhyme is lousy
and your rhythm's no good.
We'll tear it apart and
make it sound like it should."

Criticism is fine
I can take it well enough
but I can't stand
this destructive stuff.

I liked that poem,
it was part of me.
And if you don't like this one,
just let it be!!

—*Carl Kromminga*

FOR A STUDENT SLEEPING IN A POETRY WORKSHOP

I've watched his eyelids sag, spring open
  Vaguely and gradually go sliding
    Shut again, fly up
With a kind of drunken surprise, then wobble
  Peacefully together to send him
    Home from one school early. Soon his lashes
Flutter in REM sleep. I suppose he's dreaming
  What all of us kings and poets and peasants
    Have dreamed: of not making the grade,
Of draining the inexhaustible horn cup
  Of the cerebral cortex where ganglions
    Are ganging up on us with more connections
Than atoms in heaven, but coming up once more
  Empty. I see a clear stillness
    Settle over his face, a calming of the surface
Of water when the wind dies. Somewhere
  Down there, he's taking another course
    Whose resonance (let's hope) resembles
The muttered thunder, the gutter bowling, the lightning
  Of minor minions of Thor, the groans and gurgling
    Of feral lovers and preliterate Mowglis, the songs

Of shamans whistled through bird bones. A worried neighbor
   Gives him the elbow, and he shudders
      Awake, recollects himself, brings back
His hands from aboriginal outposts,
   Takes in new light, reorganizes his shoes,
      Stands up in them at the buzzer, barely recalls
His books and notebooks, meets my eyes
   And wonders what to say and whether to say it,
      Then keeps it to himself as today's lesson.

— David Wagoner

PROFESSIONAL DEVELOPMENT

My first year of college teaching,
a visiting assistant professor.
And my own office — or half of one —
in a stately red-brick edifice
with a white wooden cupola,
looking out on the autumn hills.

And I, at my desk, lavishing
a freshman essay with comment
after helpful comment, like
so many leaves coming to rest
upon the margins of each thought.

That is when my mentor, the poet,
looked over my shoulder and said,
"Son, you're putting chrome
wheels on a manure spreader."

—Paul Willis

CLASS OUTSIDE

It's never as good as students think
it will be: even in Arcadia
weed-whackers whine
in a hover above our voices.

The professor gets grass
stains on his khaki seat,
and half the class is gone
when a girl in white shorts walks by.

Even when it kind of works, the wind
keeps turning pages, a mosquito
gets smeared across the *Georgics*,
a ladybug lands in someone's tea.

But every spring we are back
out here on the grass, ringed
on the green, posing
for university photographers,

and squinting to read in the glare
of the sun's brand new flesh.

—Benjamin Myers

THE CORRESPONDENCE SCHOOL INSTRUCTOR
SAYS GOODBYE TO HIS POETRY STUDENTS

Goodbye, lady in Bangor, who sent me
snapshots of yourself, after definitely hinting
you were beautiful; goodbye,
Miami Beach urologist, who enclosed plain
brown envelopes for the return of your *very*
"Clinical Sonnets"; goodbye, manufacturer
of brassieres on the Coast, whose eclogues
give the fullest treatment in literature yet
to the sagging breast motif; goodbye, you in San Quentin,
who wrote, "Being German my hero is Hitler,"
instead of "Sincerely yours," at the end of long
neat-scripted letters demolishing
the pre-Raphaelites:

I swear to you, it was just my way
of cheering myself up, as I licked
the stamped, self-addressed envelopes,
the game I had
of trying to guess which one of you, this time,
had poisoned his glue. I did care.
I did read each poem entire.
I did say what I thought was the truth
in the mildest words I knew. And now,
in this poem, or chopped prose, not any better,
I realize, than those troubled lines
I kept sending back to you,
I have to say I am relieved it is over:

at the end I could feel only pity
for that urge toward more life
your poems kept smothering in words, the smell
of which, days later, would tingle
in your nostrils as new, God-given impulses
to write.

Goodbye,
you who are, for me, the postmarks again
of shattered towns — Xenia, Burnt Cabins, Hornell —
their loneliness
given away in poems, only their solitude kept.

— Galway Kinnell

WORKSHOP

I might as well begin by saying how much I like the title.
It gets me right away because I'm in a workshop now
so immediately the poem has my attention,
like the Ancient Mariner grabbing me by the sleeve.

And I like the first couple of stanzas,
the way they establish this mode of self-pointing
that runs through the whole poem
and tells us that words are food thrown down
on the ground for other words to eat.
I can almost taste the tail of the snake
in its own mouth,
if you know what I mean.

But what I'm not sure about is the voice,
which sounds in places very casual, very blue jeans,
but other times seems standoffish,
professorial in the worst sense of the word
like the poem is blowing pipe smoke in my face.
But maybe that's just what it wants to do.

What I did find engaging were the middle stanzas,
especially the fourth one.
I like the image of clouds flying like lozenges
which gives me a very clear picture.
And I really like how this drawbridge operator
just appears out of the blue
with his feet up on the iron railing
and his fishing pole jigging—I like jigging—

a hook in the slow industrial canal below.
I love slow industrial canal below. All those *l*'s.

Maybe it's just me,
but the next stanza is where I start to have a problem.
I mean how can the evening bump into the stars?
And what's an obbligato of snow?
Also, I roam the decaffeinated streets.
At that point I'm lost. I need help.

The other thing that throws me off,
and maybe this is just me,
is the way the scene keeps shifting around.
First, we're in this big aerodrome
and the speaker is inspecting a row of dirigibles,
which makes me think this could be a dream.
Then he takes us into his garden,
the part with the dahlias and the coiling hose,
though that's nice, the coiling hose,
but then I'm not sure where we're supposed to be.
The rain and the mint green light,
that makes it feel outdoors, but what about this wallpaper?
Or is it a kind of indoor cemetery?
There's something about death going on here.

In fact, I start to wonder if what we have here
is really two poems, or three, or four,
or possibly none.

But then there's that last stanza, my favorite.
This is where the poem wins me back,
especially the lines spoken in the voice of the mouse.
I mean we've all seen these images in cartoons before,
but I still love the details he uses
when he's describing where he lives.
The perfect little arch of an entrance in the baseboard,
the bed made out of a curled-back sardine can,
the spool of thread for a table.
I start thinking about how hard the mouse had to work
night after night collecting all these things
while the people in the house were fast asleep,
and that gives me a very strong feeling,
a very powerful sense of something.
But I don't know if anyone else was feeling that.
Maybe that was just me.
Maybe that's just the way I read it.

—Billy Collins

THE ENGLISH TEACHER CONTEMPLATES SUICIDE

but first has to scribe a note
worthy of publication: the stress
of addressing the intelligentsia,
balancing wit and wisdom,
practicing the prose she preaches
paralyzes her. Posthumous

is the way to go, yet
unmixing metaphors is so
mortifying, unconstructing
deconstruction undoable
in a day, much less
those meticulous minutes
it takes to pen
a well performed and poetic

Help! pitiful but pithy enough
for any Plath-loving
parishioner. She breathes
deeply, chooses a pad,
skillfully researches all
inner resources but everything's
checked out. After three

wastebaskets of would-be
winsome epistles, she settles
for near-death, takes up the red pen
once again to mark.

—Marjorie Maddox

HUMANITIES COURSE

Professor Varder handles Dante
  With wry respect; while one can see
It's all a lie, one must admit
  The "beauty" of the "imagery."

Professor Varder slyly smiles,
  Describing Hegel as a "sage";
But still, the man has value—he
  Reflects the "temper" of his "age."

Montaigne, Tom Paine, St. Augustine:
  Although their notions came to naught,
They still are "crucial figures" in
  The "pageantry" of "Western thought."

—John Updike

ABSENT-MINDED PROFESSOR

This lonely figure of not much fun
Strayed out of folklore fifteen years ago
Forever. Now on an autumn afternoon,
While the leaves drift past the office window,
His bright replacement, present-minded, stays
At the desk correcting papers, nor ever grieves,
For the silly scholar of the bad old days,
Who'd burn the papers and correct the leaves.

—Howard Nemerov

MR. ATTILA

They made a myth of you, professor,
      you of the gentle voice,
      the books, the specs,
      the furtive rabbit manners
      in the mortar-board cap
      and the medieval gown.

They didn't think it, eh professor?
On account of you're so absent-minded,
you bumping into the tree and saying,
"Excuse me, I thought you were a tree,"
passing on again blank and absent-minded.

Now it's "Mr. Attila, *how* do you do?"
Do you pack wallops of wholesale death?
Are you the practical dynamic son-of-a-gun?
Have you come through with a few abstractions?
Is it you Mr. Attila we hear saying,
"I beg your pardon but we believe we have made some degree
of progress
      on the residual qualities of the atom"?

—Carl Sandburg

AN ENGLISH TEACHER

After a summer of beaches Mr. Meeching,
Dressed as always in flannel and bristling tweed,
Applied his tanned physique again to teaching
Shelley and Meeching and how to (romantically) bleed.

Standing before his first class with the erotic
Air of the Cape still curling his hair,
He thought of the sand and the breakers, and of an exotic
Quohaug chowder with camembert.

Abstracted, class roll in hand, he let his gaze wander
Lazily out over thirty-three heads to a dim
Window where trees became masts and grass water
And lobsters crawled on the steps of the briny gym.

Sadly recalled to the roll, the text and the faces,
He saw stretched before him a continent of drab
And merely poetic commonplaces
With nary a long-necked clam or soft-shelled crab.

Poor Meeching.
Would he ever again get through to the ocean side?
He doubted it.
Having no thoughts to comfort his soul in his dark night of teaching
Except that lucky old Shelley (by drowning) died.

—Reed Whittemore

ANOTHER TEACHER

He hated them all one by one but wanted to show them
What was important and vital and by God if
They thought they'd never have use for it he was
Sorry as hell for them, that's all, with their genteel
Mercantile Main Street Babbitt
Bourgeois-barbaric faces, they were beyond
Saving, clearly, quite out of reach, and so he
G-rrr
Got up every morning and g-rrr ate his breakfast
And g-rrr lumbered off to his eight o'clock
Gladly to teach.

—*Reed Whittemore*

ON FLUNKING A NICE BOY OUT OF SCHOOL

I wish I could teach you how ugly
decency and humility can be when they are not
the election of a contained mind but only
the defenses of an incompetent. Were you taught
meekness as a weapon? Or did you discover,
by chance maybe, that it worked on mother
and was generally a good thing—
at least when all also failed—to get you over
the worst of what was coming. Is that why
you bring these sheepfaces to Tuesday?

                                                         They won't do.
It's three months work I want, and I'd sooner have it
from the brassiest lumpkin in pimpledom, but have it,
than all these martyred repentances from you.

—John Ciardi

ZIMMER'S HEAD THUDDING AGAINST THE BLACKBOARD

At the blackboard I had missed
Five number problems in a row,
And was about to foul a sixth,
When the old, exasperated nun
Began to pound my head against
My six mistakes. When I cried,
She threw me back into my seat,
Where I hid my head and swore
That very day I'd be a poet,
And curse her yellow teeth with this.

—Paul Zimmer

IV

from *The Canterbury Tales*
THE GENERAL PROLOGUE

A Clerk ther was of Oxenforde also
That unto logic hadde longe ygo.
As lene was his hors as is a rake,
And he was nought right fat, I undertake,
But looked holwe, and therto sobrely.
Ful thredbare was his overeste courtepy,
For he hadde geten him yit no benefice,
Ne was so worldly for to have office,
For him was levere have at his beddes heed
Twenty bookes, clad in blak or reed,
Of Aristotle and his philosophye,
Than robes riche, or fithele, or gay sautrye.
But al be that he was a philosopher
Yit hadde he but litel gold in cofre;
But al that he mighte of his frendes hente,
On bookes and on learning he it spente,
And bisily gan fior the soules praye
Of hem that yaf him wherewith to scoleye.
Of studye took he most cure and most heede.
Noughtoo word spajk he more than was neede,
And that was said in forme and reverence,
And short and quik, and ful of heigh sentence;
Souning in moral vertu was his speeche,
And gladly wolde he lerne, and gladly teche.

— Geoffrey Chaucer

PERENNIALS

May sunshine, and the old professor
sits his deck
eating a cold beef sandwich
while just above the grass
the sparrows trampoline
wind currents as if they're
guided by remote control.

The wren's so happy
he can't contain himself
and the house finch flits
from tree to bush, her neck
bright red against the green.

"I could sit here all afternoon," he thinks,
"listening and looking."

This morning he read
a freshman paper which told him
that "old people are waiting for death
and content with their surroundings."

Most of the perennials
have sent out shoots of green.
He imagines them slowly growing,
eating rain and sunshine
to stack cells one against another,
calmly working toward a flower,
pushing up, up.

—David Schelhaas

REQUIEM: PROFESSOR WALT MINK (1927-1996)

My friend's eyelids were closed
with these thumbs, which left
faint whirlpools of skin oil.
It's okay. He'd stopped
seeing: The lifelong film unreeling behind his gaze
had stopped (sprocket jam, gear freeze, dim

to black). So the last frame burned out
(as I picture it) white on the brain's bulb.
No one could fix it, though this friend was a scientist,
and I'd watched his hands repair
the skull circuits of mice small as my thumb.
That was in my youth and in his tutelage.

And everyone he touched
seemed changed by it—brighter, faster, more
capable of love. Thinking of him
I feel pliable again.
I long for hands imbued
with grace to shape me.

And I worry the form I'll finally take (death
lesson) and whether I can be made to leave
on anyone some mark worth bearing.

—*Mary Karr*

WINTER TERM'S END

The student pokes her head into my cubicle.
She's climbed the screw-thread stairs that spiral up
to the crow's nest where I work
to say goodbye.
She hands back books I lent.
I wave her to move papers from the spot

she always took, worrying a sentence or a line;
or come with protruded tongue to show
a silver stud;
or bamboozled by some guy who can't appreciate
the dragon tattooed on her breast, the filigree
around her thigh. This term she's done with school.

Four years she's siphoned every phrase,
or anecdote, or quote that's mine to dole.
She knows what I know;
or used to know, for in me sonnets fade.
Homer erodes
like sandstone worn by age.

Each year I grow emptier, more obsolete,
can barely grope
to words that once hung iridescent in my skull.
When, thirty years back, I asked my beloved tutor
how I'd ever pay him back, he said, *It's not*
that linear. Only carry on this talk

with someone else.
All his thoughts on Western Civ
would melt like ice without this kid—
hair dyed torch red, painted flames on her lug-sole boots.
She safety-pinned a plastic charm
of Our Lady's sacred heart to her sleeve.

Last night, to plot her destiny
she hurled at the world map a lopsided dart
and hit a South Seas flyspeck. Call collect,
I say, if you get stuck. Read
thus-and-such translation of Rilke *only*.
And though I sound like Polonius to myself,

she scribbles down my platitudes.
Without her like,
I'd live in the dull smear
of my own profession, each kid
a repeat, indistinct from the vanishing instants
that mark us made.

The hand that holds this pen's assembled by some force
newly manifest
in her face. She brought amazement for a spell,
then tore loose into the labyrinth I've meandered in
addled as a child, feeling along the string my teacher tied.
My eyes stare out from ever deeper sockets, edged in mesh.

I watch her cross the snow-swirled quad
backpacked in hunter plaid, bent like an old scholar,
moving with care across the slippery earth.
Snow is falling
over the quad, like rare pages
shredded and dispersed by wind,

that wild white filling every place we've stepped.

(for Betsy Hogan)

—Mary Karr

THE TEACHER

I was twenty-six the first time I held
a human heart in my hand.

It was sixty-four and heavier than I expected,
its chambers slack;
and I was stupidly surprised
at how cold it was.

It was the middle of the third week
before I could look at her face,
before I could spend more than an hour
learning the secrets of cirrhosis,
the dark truth of diabetes, the black lungs
of the Marlboro woman, the exquisite
painful shape of kidney stones,
without eating an entire box of Altoids
to smother the smell of formaldehyde.

After seeing her face, I could not help
but wonder if she had a favorite color;
if she hated beets,
or loved country music before her hearing
faded, or learned to read
before cataracts placed her in perpetual twilight.
I wondered if her mother had once been happy
when she'd come home from school
or if she'd ever had a valentine from a secret admirer.

In the weeks that followed, I would
drive the highways, scanning billboards.
I would see her face, her eyes
squinting away the cigarette smoke,
or she would turn up at the bus stop
pushing a grocery cart of empty
beer cans and soda bottles. I wondered
if that was how she'd paid for all those smokes
or if the scars of repeated infections in her womb
spoke to a more universal currency.

Did she die, I wondered, in a cardboard box
under the Burnside Bridge, nursing a bottle
of strawberry wine, telling herself
she felt a little warmer now,
or in the Good Faith Shelter,
her few belongings safe under the sheet
held to her faltering heart?
Or in the emergency room, lying
on a wheeled gurney, the pitiless
lights above, the gauzy curtains around?

Did she ever wonder what it all was for?

I wish I could have told her in those days
what I've now come to know that
it was for this — the baring
of her body on the stainless steel table —
that I might come to know its secrets
and, knowing them, might listen
to the machine-shop hum of aortic stenosis

in an old woman's chest, smile a little to myself
and, in gratitude to her who taught me,

put away my stethoscope, turn to my patient
and say *Let's talk about your heart.*

—*Hilarie Jones*

THE TEACHER'S REWARD

After the last lecture before exam week
she came down into the pit,
waiting her turn behind those who
wanted to hear what they had to know
for the final.

I was always tempted to say,
"Nothing, it's up to you, it's your education."
But that would have taken longer,
and wouldn't have made any sense
at the time, anyway.

And I didn't know her from Eve
because I had 673 students,
I'll call them,
in three lecture sections.
She was not someone I had met.

She was not the one who had told me,
"Your exam wasn't fair, it made us think."

Or the one whose mom was planning to come
for graduation and,
"Is there anything I can do to make up for
missing every mid-term and lab quiz?"

Or the one whose coach wanted to know
if there was any way the seven-footer
whose name I can't remember
could pass.

The class was 9 T-Th in sched talk
and she was a senior taking this
100-level exercise in general zoology
just to fill a chuck hole
on her otherwise macadam-smooth
road to graduation.

Her only T-Th obligation,
one she hadn't missed all semester, she said.
She wanted me to know that,
then hurried away before I could ask
her name, which I wouldn't have anyway.

—David Wright

THE LAST CLASS

They crowd near. If you look at them
they look down. Pause. They shuffle their feet.
Over near the windows along one side
patches of light shine on the floor.
It is almost the hour to begin
whatever comes after this day.

Over their heads you see so many
clouds and stars and days. A hook
begins to come down from the sky.
If you call out, if you warn them,
what good will it do? It is the long
moment that always opens at such times.

Now the eyes turn away. A new
high-pitched hum has compelled the others
to look around. What happens next?
You look toward the exit; this isn't
your place any more. It was coming,
now it is here, the call. Not for them—

For you. It is for you.

—William Stafford

ON THE DEATH OF A COLLEAGUE

She taught theater, so we gathered
in the theater.
We praised her voice, her knowledge,
how good she was
with *Godot* and just four months later
with *Gigi*.
She was fifty. The problem in the liver.
Each of us recalled
an incident in which she'd been kind
or witty.
I told about being unable to speak
from my diaphragm
and how she made me lie down, placed her hand
where the failure was
and showed me how to breathe.
But afterwards
I only could do it when I lay down
and that became a joke
between us, and I told it as my offering
to the audience.
I was on stage and I heard myself
wishing to be impressive.
Someone else spoke of her cats
and no one spoke
of her face or the last few parties.
The fact was
I had avoided her for months.

It was a student's turn to speak, a sophomore,
one of her actors.
She was a drunk, he said, often came to class
reeking.
Sometimes he couldn't look at her, the blotches,
the awful puffiness.
And yet she was a great teacher,
he loved her,
but thought someone should say
what everyone knew
because she didn't die by accident.

Everyone was crying. Everyone was crying and it
was almost over now.
The remaining speaker, an historian, said he'd cut
his speech short.
And the Chairman stood up as if by habit,
said something about loss
and thanked us for coming. None of us moved
except some students
to the student who'd spoken, and then others
moved to him, across dividers,
down aisles, to his side of the stage.

—Stephen Dunn

FOR WGF
WHO WAS TOLD HE DIDN'T PUBLISH
ENOUGH TO BE PROMOTED TO ASSOCIATE
PROFESSOR

The hell with universities!
For us, long ago
you were an associate professor of gentleness
who could play for us
the music we didn't
know how much we wanted to hear.

In the journal of gaiety
you published for us
                                entire nights!
that we will always
acknowledge in the obscure articles
our hearts may write.

Do you remember telling us
about the Highland Scots of 1746
—strange men with old loyalties—
blowing their bagpipes, marching
from the hills
to be slaughtered on an open field
by the modern world's artillery?

                        They live in all of us. We

don't want the new king. But
this time—let the British
keep the lowlands. We'll stay
in the mountains, preaching,
singing, weaving and propagating
our own kind.

—Lou Lipsitz

WHAT TEACHERS MAKE, OR OBJECTION OVERRULED, OR IF THINGS DON'T WORK OUT, YOU CAN ALWAYS GO TO LAW SCHOOL

He says the problem with teachers is,
What's a kid going to learn from someone
who decided his best option in life was to become a teacher?
He reminds the other dinner guests that it's true
what they say about teachers:
Those who can, do; those who can't, teach.
I decide to bite my tongue—instead of his—
and resist the temptation to remind the other dinner guests
that it's also true what they say about lawyers.
Because we're eating, after all, and this is a polite conversation.

I mean, you're a teacher, Taylor.
Be honest. What do you make?

And I wish he hadn't done that—asked me to be honest—
Because, you see, I have a policy
about honesty and ass-kicking:
if you ask for it, I have to let you have it.
You want to know what I make?

I make kids work harder than they ever thought they could.
I can make a C+ feel like a Congressional Medal of Honor
and an A- feel like a slap in the face.
How dare you waste my time with anything less than your very best.

I make kids sit through 40 minutes of study hall
in absolute silence. *No, you may not work in groups.*
No, you may not ask a question.
Why won't I let you go to the bathroom?
Because you're bored.
And you don't really have to go to the bathroom, do you?

I make parents tremble in fear when I call home:
Hi, This is Mr. Mali. I hope I haven't called at a bad time,
I just wanted to talk to you about something your son said today.
To the biggest bully in the grade, he said, "Leave the kid alone.
I still cry sometimes, don't you? It's no big deal."
And it was the noblest act of courage I have ever seen.
I make parents see their children for who they are
and what they can be.

You want to know what I make?

I make kids wonder,
I make them question.
I make them criticize.
I make them apologize and mean it.
I make them write, write, write,
and then I make them read.
I make them spell
definitely beautiful, definitely beautiful,
definitely beautiful over and over again until they will never misspell
either one of those words again.
I make them show all their work in math,
and hide it on their final drafts in English.
I make them understand that if you got *this*

then you follow *this*,
and if someone ever tries to judge you
by what you make, you give them *this*.

Here, let me break it down for you,
so you know what I say is true:
Teachers? Teachers make a difference!
Now what about you?

— Taylor Mali

FINAL EXAM

Outside 201 a locker door clangs,
Wind from the west shivers window slats.
Behind my Navy-gray desk I await
Three final exams for AP Brit Lit.
        Graduation rehearsal at 4 in the gym.
        Mandatory for seniors and faculty.

Ava lays her bluebook on the stack,
Squares it with purple nails, mouths, "Thank you!!"
In the hall she shrieks, long and thrillingly,
Her sandals slap-slapping away.
        The bosun's pipe trills. Set the sea detail.
        Single up fore and aft. Take in all lines.

The clock above me clicks to 3:09.
Calendar leaves flutter, May, June, May, June
In the west window breeze. Outside two guys
Toss a football in the parking lot.
        Summer school classes start June 17.
        See your counselor to register.

Waiting, I slide open ENGLISH LIT bin
And file two copies in AP EXAM.
Behind owl glasses Gordon looks up,
Nods, resumes for ten extra credit points.
        Pilot's on the bridge. Rudder amidships.
        Back one-third on port. All engines stop.

"How has reading poetry changed you?"
His profs will love him. Gina writes on,
Frowning, twisting a strand. She can go
Anywhere — if she dumps that loser guy.
      Grades must be recorded in Academic File
      By tomorrow noon, failing seniors today.

I push back, stand up. "Time to wrap up now!"
They hand over the last two exams and
I stuff the stack into my pack.
At the door Gordon turns back,
      "Thanks, doc. Have a good summer!"
      "You, too, Gordon. Good luck at Kenyon!"

Not ready to go ashore, I stash mug
In left top drawer, thermos in pack.
Erase white board. Toss Senior Home Room list.
Scan staff memo: Re September Schedule
      August 3o, all faculty report.
      Welcome aboard new faculty and staff!

Tomorrow and tomorrow and tomorrow.
Tear off June and July. Circle August 3o.
Summer's lease hath all too short a date.
A week at Sea Ranch, then back on deck.
      With breakwater light abeam come left
      To 165. Left to 165, aye.

Ocean swells roll in from the west,
Shiver the bow, hiss along the hull.
Clear of the harbor she takes up
The slow steady roll of ocean swells.
       The Captain has the con. On deck
       The underway watch. Steady as she goes.

—J. Barry Koops

COMMENCEMENT

I sneak back to campus, summer Saturday.
Someone has left Porter Hall open.
I stand at the lectern, fill the empty
Rows with freshmen,
Whisper the first words of my opening lecture,
And the room gets smaller,

Like my third grade playground,
Where it seemed miles from the fence
To Miss Tillinger
Who blew her whistle to retrieve us,
All crewcuts and ponytails, Karens and Bills,
Endowed with time to cross vast distances,

Like the hundred yards here to my old office
Where I peek through blinds
At the latest occupant's scholarly stacks:
A thousand familiar volumes, thick with knowing,
But almost none, as I recall,
Contain pictures.

No whistle sounds, but I know that
Despite my inconspicuously professorial appearance,
Lingering
Will get me sent to the principal's office for sure,
So I climb the hill to the parking lot—
Not as steep as I remembered—and drive away,
Red-eyed, to the grownups.

— Thomas Schmidt

LINES ON RETIREMENT
AFTER READING LEAR

Avoid storms. And retirement parties.
You can't trust the sweetnesses your friends will
offer, when they really want your office,
which they'll redecorate. Beware the still
untested pension plan. Keep your keys. Ask
for more troops than you think you'll need. Listen
more to fools and less to colleagues. Love your
youngest child the most, regardless. Back to
storms: dress warm, take a friend, don't eat the grass,
don't stand near tall trees, and keep the yelling
down—the winds won't listen, and no one will
see you in the dark. It's too hard to hear
you over all the thunder. But you're not
Lear, except that we can't stop you from what
you've planned to do. In the end, no one leaves
the stage in character—we never see
the feather, the mirror held to our lips.
So don't wait for skies to crack with sun. Feel
the storm's sweet sting invade you to the skin,
the strange, sore comforts of the wind. Embrace
your children's ragged praise and that of friends.
Go ahead, take it off, take it all off.
Run naked into tempests. Weave flowers
into your hair. Bellow at cataracts.
If you dare, scream at the gods. Babble as
if you thought words could save. Drink rain like cold
beer. So much better than making theories.
We'd all come with you, laughing, if we could.

—David Wright

THE SCHOLARS

Bald heads forgetful of their sins,
Old, learned, respectable bald heads
Edit and annotate the lines
That young men, tossing on their beds,
Rhymed out in love's despair
To flatter beauty's ignorant ear.

All shuffle there; all cough in ink;
All wear the carpet with their shoes;
All think what other people think;
All know the man their neighbor knows.
Lord, what would they say
Did their Catullus walk that way?

— William Butler Yeats

REACH

for my students

Between black clouds, late fierce light slants
A threat of storm on grass
That students and scholars do not trod.
No, we respect the paths made for us.

This is the same grass I did not trod
In a Cambridge courtyard
Where Isaac Newton once measured
The speed of sound. I kept to paths.

Now, in the interval between flash and boom,
I calculate that none of us is far
From the apple of gravity that drops
Near enough the path to reach.

— Thomas Schmidt

25TH HIGH SCHOOL REUNION

We come to hear the endings
of all the stories
in our anthology
of false starts:
how the girl who seemed
as hard as nails
was hammered
into shape;
how the athletes ran
out of races;
how under the skin
our skulls rise
to the surface
like rocks in the bed
of a drying stream.
Look! We have all
turned into
ourselves.

— Linda Pastan

GRATITUDE TO OLD TEACHERS

When we stride or stroll across the frozen lake,
We place our feet where they have never been.
We walk upon the unwalked. But we are uneasy.
Who is down there but our old teachers?

Water that once could take no human weight—
We were students then—holds up our feet,
And goes on ahead of us for a mile.
Beneath us the teachers, and around us the stillness.

—Robert Bly

ABOUT THE POETS

Robert Bly (b. 1926) grew up in Minnesota. After two years
in the Navy, he attended St. Olaf College before transferring
to Harvard, where he associated with others who became
successful poets: Donald Hall, Adrienne Rich, John Ashbery.
He studied for two years at the University of Iowa Writers'
Workshop. Bly opposed the Vietnam War with his influence
and poems. Later in life he was a spokesperson for the "men's
movement"; his book *Iron John* was a significant cultural force.
For more, see www.robertbly.com.

Gwendolyn Brooks (1917-2000) was born in Topeka, Kansas,
but her family moved to Chicago where she lived the rest of her
life. She began writing in her early teens, eventually publishing
20 volumes of poems, many about fellow African Americans in
her urban community. Widely praised and honored, Brooks
received the Pulitzer Prize and was named consultant to the
Library of Congress (now known as poet laureate) and poet
laureate of the state of Illinois. Her contribution to American
letters included teaching extensively at universities around the
country.

Sietse Buning is the pen name of Stanley Wiersma (1930-
1986), who grew up in a Dutch Calvinist farming community in
northwest Iowa. Wiersma attended Calvin College and earned
his BA. He taught high school English for a year and then
served in the U.S. Army in Japan. He earned an MS and PhD at
University of Wisconsin-Madison. Wiersma returned to Calvin,
his alma mater, where he taught in the English Department for
27 years – beloved by faculty and students alike.

Herm Card (b. 1947) is a former Syracuse University baseball player and coach, retired NCAA umpire, and a member of the New York State Public High School Athletic Association Hall of Fame. A retired English teacher, he has worked for the National Baseball Hall of Fame, The Eagle Newspapers and the New York State Senate, and has won awards for his teaching, officiating, photography and poetry. Card is currently an adjunct professor in the Sports Media Department of the S.I. Newhouse School of Public Communication.

Brenda Cárdenas (b. 1965) lives in Milwaukee, Wisconsin, the city of her birth. She received a BA from the University of Wisconsin–Milwaukee and an MFA from the University of Michigan. She is the author of two volumes of poetry, *Boomerang* and *From the Tongues of Brick and Stone*. Cárdenas writes in a blend of English and Spanish. She served as the Milwaukee poet laureate from 2010 to 2012, and currently teaches in the creative writing program at the University of Wisconsin–Milwaukee.

Charles Causley (1917-2003) was born and brought up in Launceston, Cornwall, UK and lived there most of his life. During World War II he served in the Royal Navy aboard a destroyer. His poetry was recognized by the Queen's Gold Medal for Poetry and a Cholmondeley Award. In addition to these honors, Causley was greatly respected by his peers in the world of literature. At the same time, his poetry, especially the ballads, had a wide popularity, and among his countrymen he was beloved.

Geoffrey Chaucer (1343-1400), author of *The Canterbury Tales*, is the greatest English poet of the Middle Ages. Born in London, Chaucer was a civil servant, courtier, and diplomat. He served as controller of customs for the port of London and later as clerk of the king's works. His wife, Philippa, was a lady-in-waiting to the queen. For his service—and possibly his poetry—Edward III awarded him "a gallon of wine a day for the rest of his life." Chaucer's Tales and poems, appearing at a time of growing literacy, were popular. His remains were buried in Westminster Abbey.

John Ciardi (1916-1986) was a poet, translator, and etymologist. He translated Dante's *Divine Comedy*, and wrote several volumes of children's poetry. His long-time position as columnist and poetry editor of the *Saturday Review* gave him both popularity and notoriety for his sometimes acerbic observations and verse. He taught at Harvard and at Middlebury College in Vermont, where he directed the Bread Loaf Writers' Conference. Following its publication in 1975, Ciardi's book *How Does a Poem Mean?* was among the most-used literature textbooks of its time. In the early 1960s he also hosted a network television program, *Accent*, on CBS.

Billy Collins (b. 1941) grew up mainly in Queens, New York. He is the author of 12 collections of poetry, most recently, *The Rain in Portugal*. A Distinguished Professor of English at Lehman College of the City University of New York, he was poet laureate of the United States and New York State Poet. In 2016 he was inducted into the American Academy of Arts and Letters. Collins may be the most widely read and popular poet since Robert Frost.

Diane Dawber (b. 1946) earned a Master of Education degree from Queen's University and now writes near Kingston, Ontario. Among her whimsically named children's books are *Oatmeal Mittens*, *How Do You Wrestle a Goldfish?* and *My Cake's on Fire!* She has also edited anthologies and written poetry and books for health-conscious adults. Having survived a disabling illness, she now does public lectures on dealing with pain and fatigue.

Carl Dennis (b. 1939), born in St. Louis, lives in Buffalo, New York. He taught at the State University of New York–Buffalo for 35 years, where he was a professor of English and writer in residence. Dennis has published 12 books of poetry, including *Night School*, his most recent. His work has received numerous awards, and many of his poems have appeared in The *New Yorker*.

Toi Derricotte (b. 1941), born in Hamtramck, Michigan, received her early education at Detroit's Girls Catholic Central High School. She earned her BA in special education from Wayne State University and her MA in English literature from New York University. Derricotte has received numerous honors and awards for her five collections of poetry. She co-founded the Cave Canem Foundation, which is committed to cultivating the artistic and professional growth of African American poets. She teaches at the University of Pittsburgh. For more, see www.toiderricotte.com.

Dante Di Stefano (b. 1978) is the author of two poetry collections: *Love Is a Stone Endlessly in Flight* and *Ill Angels*. Along with María Isabel Álvarez, he co-edited the anthology

Misrepresented People: Poetic Responses to Trump's America. He holds a PhD from Binghamton University and teaches 10th and 12th grade English in upstate New York.

Brian Doyle (1956-2017) was born in New York City and grew up in a large Irish Catholic family. Doyle earned a degree in English from the University of Notre Dame. Thereafter, his day jobs were at magazines: *U.S. Catholic, Boston College Magazine* and finally *Portland Magazine*, which he edited until his death. A novelist, essayist, poet, and editor, he was honored with the American Academy of Arts and Letters Award in Literature, a Catholic Book Award, three Pushcart Prizes and the John Burroughs Medal for Distinguished Nature Writing.

Stephen Dunn (b. 1939) was born in Forest Hills, New York. He attended Hofstra University on a basketball scholarship and later worked in advertising. He earned an MA in creative writing from Syracuse University. Dunn is the author of 16 books of poetry, including *Different Hours* for which he was awarded the Pulitzer Prize. Since 1974 he has taught at Richard Stockton College of New Jersey. Dunn's work has appeared in magazines, including *The New Yorker*, *The Atlantic*, *The Nation*, and *The New Republic*.

Maura Eichner (1915-2009) was born in Brooklyn, New York and was educated in the School Sisters of Notre Dame, which order she joined at 18. She hoped to dedicate her life to teaching young children, preferably the poor. However, she was assigned to the English Department at the College of Notre Dame of Maryland, where she taught with distinction for 50 years. Eichner published ten books of poetry, including

What We Women Know and *Hope Is a Blind Bard*. She inspired generations of students with love of poetry and writing.

Louise Erdrich (b. 1954) was born in Little Falls, Minnesota. As the daughter of a Chippewa Indian mother and a German-American father, Erdrich explores Native-American themes in her works, with major characters from both sides of her heritage. Erdrich attended Dartmouth College and earned an MA at Johns Hopkins University. She published three volumes of poems and many best-selling novels. She lives in Minneapolis and operates Birchbark Books, an independent bookstore.

Peter Everwine (1930-2018) was born in Detroit and raised in western Pennsylvania. He published seven collections of poetry, which earned multiple awards and honors. His poetry has been featured in the *Paris Review* and the *American Poetry Review*, among others. He also translated poetry from the Hebrew and Aztec languages. Everwine taught at Reed College and at California State University in Fresno, where he lived.

Jane Flanders (1940-2001), poet and musician, was born in Waynesboro, Pennsylvania and lived there until leaving for Bryn Mawr College. After two years teaching English at the Punahou School in Hawaii she obtained an MA in English at Columbia University. At various times she taught at the University of Pittsburgh and other institutions. Flanders is the author of four books of poems; her work is warmly praised by her peers. At her death in 2001 she left almost 700 unpublished poems.

Isabella Gardner (1915-1981) was born into a patrician New England family (her mother a Grosvenor, her father a Peabody) and she was named for the great-aunt who bequeathed a museum in Boston. She was educated in private schools and studied acting in London. After a period of professional acting, Gardner moved to Chicago, where she married a McCormick and served as an associate editor of *Poetry* magazine. Gardner published four volumes during her lifetime, and her work appeared in prestigious journals: *Poetry*, *Partisan Review*, *Paris Review*, *The New Yorker*, and *The Atlantic*.

Louise Glück (b. 1943) was born in New York City and grew up on Long Island. She attended, but did not graduate from, Sarah Lawrence College and Columbia University. Her poems are both personal and mythical, often about relationships—especially marriage and family. Glück has published 15 books of poems and a prize-winning volume of essays. In 2003 she was named the 12th U.S. poet laureate, succeeding Billy Collins. In recognition of her highly regarded art and craft she has been awarded a long list of prizes and awards. Glück is currently writer-in-residence at Yale University.

Seamus Heaney (1939-2013) is widely recognized as one of the major poets of the 20th century. A Catholic in (Protestant) Northern Ireland, he knew "the troubles" first hand. He was the author of over 20 volumes of poetry and criticism, and he translated classics, as well as "Beowulf" from Anglo-Saxon. He won the Nobel Prize for Literature "for works of lyrical beauty and ethical depth, which exalt everyday miracles and the living past." Heaney taught at Harvard University and served as the Oxford Professor of Poetry.

Edward Hirsch (b. 1950) was born in Chicago and educated at Grinnell College and the University of Pennsylvania, where he received a PhD in Folklore. He has published seven books of poems over 35 years of writing. Hirsch taught at Wayne State University and then for 17 years in the Creative Writing Program at the University of Houston. Hirsch's book, *How to Read a Poem and Fall in Love with Poetry*, was a bestseller and is widely taught. He is now president of the John Simon Guggenheim Memorial Foundation, a post from which he supports artists and scientists. For more, see www.edwardhirsch.com.

Andrew Hudgins (b. 1951) was born into a military family and, growing up, moved around the American South, settling eventually in Montgomery, Alabama. He earned an MFA at the Iowa Writers Workshop. His poems that deal with folk myths, jokes, religion, and small-town and rural life bring to mind the Southern literary tradition; his book *The Glass Hammer: A Southern Childhood* has been called a verse-autobiography. Hudgins is currently Humanities Distinguished Professor of English at the Ohio State University. He lives in Upper Arlington, Ohio, with his wife, the writer Erin McGraw.

Langston Hughes (1902-1967) was born in Joplin, Missouri and grew up in a series of mid-western towns before settling in Cleveland. He studied at Columbia University in New York City, traveled to Mexico, shipped out on a merchant ship headed to Africa, and took a variety of jobs, writing poetry all the while. In addition to his large body of poetic work, Hughes wrote 11 plays and a long list of works of prose. He lived his last decades in Harlem and was a major figure in the Harlem Renaissance.

Rod Jellema (1928-2015) grew up in Holland and Ann Arbor, Michigan; he kept close ties to the Lake Michigan shore, and images of the region appear often in his poems. Jellema was educated at Calvin College and received his PhD from the University of Edinburgh (Scotland). He taught at the University of Maryland, where he was the founding director of the Creative Writing Program. Jellema produced five books of poems, the last of which was *Incarnality: The Collected Poems*. He also translated two books of poetry from Frisian, the language of his forbears. For this work he was awarded Friesland's highest literary honor, the Pieter Jelles prize.

Hilarie Jones (b. 1956) is an acute care nurse practitioner. She studied nursing at the University of Connecticut and the University of Utah. Her clinical interests include precepting the next generation of nurse practitioners. Jones is also, in her own words, "a goat farmer, Buddhist, and dog rescuer." She says she wouldn't do anything for a Klondike bar....but she'd consider some sketchy things for some good hay.

Donald Justice (1925-2004), an accomplished poet and legendary teacher, was associated with the Iowa Writers' Workshop, where he guided a generation of poets through their early writing. Justice grew up in Florida, and earned a bachelor's degree from the University of Miami. He ultimately earned a doctorate from the University of Iowa. His *New York Times* obituary summed up Justice as "an elder of American poetry whose formalist verse and teaching skills were equally acclaimed." He was also an accomplished painter and composed music on the side.

Mary Karr (b. 1955), a poet, essayist, and raconteur, was born and raised in a tough industrial town in East Texas. Her poems frequently include personal elements, including her difficult childhood, teenage drug use, and alcoholism, as well as her recovery and conversion to Catholicism. She has published five books of poems and several volumes of prose that include memoirs, essays, and songs. Her highly regarded work has earned her many fellowships, prizes, and writing awards. Karr has taught at Syracuse University since 1991.

Jane Kenyon (1947-1995) was born in Ann Arbor, Michigan, and earned both her BA and MA from the University of Michigan. While a student at Michigan, Kenyon met her future husband, her poetry instructor Donald Hall. After her marriage to Hall, 19 years her senior, they moved to Eagle Pond Farm in New Hampshire. Kenyon published four volumes of poetry during her life, cut off at 47 by leukemia. She leaves us unsentimental, lyrical images of nature that detail the loveliness of the ordinary.

Galway Kinnell (1927-2004) grew up in Rhode Island. He served in the Navy for two years before entering Princeton University. After earning an MA from the University of Rochester, he spent several years in Europe and the Middle East. His experiences traveling abroad, working for civil rights, and protesting the Vietnam War found their way into his poetry. Kinnell was among the poets reacting against the modernism of T. S. Eliot and Ezra Pound and writing verses that, "could be understood without a graduate degree." He taught at New York University for many years.

Ron Koertge (b. 1940), a poet and novelist, grew up in rural Illinois and received a BA from the University of Illinois and an MA from the University of Arizona. Koertge is the author of numerous poetry collections including *Dairy Cows*, *Life on the Edge of the Continent: Selected Poems*, *Making Love to Roget's Wife*, and *Lies, Knives, and Girls in Red Dresses*. He also wrote several acclaimed novels, most of them for young adults. Koertge recently retired from Pasadena City College after 37 years of teaching.

J. Barry Koops (b. 1939) graduated from a mission school for Native Americans near Gallup, New Mexico. He studied English at Calvin College, where he was better known as a runner than as a scholar. After four years on a U.S. Navy ship out of Long Beach he went to the University of Michigan for an MA. Koops taught literature and writing for five years before returning to Ann Arbor for a PhD in English and education. Thereafter he served as university professor, principal, superintendent, headmaster, navigation instructor, and consultant. His poems have won minor awards. He and his wife Delianne live on a ridge overlooking San Francisco Bay.

Ted Kooser (b. 1939) is a poet and essayist, and professor of English at the University of Nebraska-Lincoln. He served as the U.S. Poet Laureate, and his book *Delights & Shadows* won the Pulitzer Prize for poetry. He worked for many years in the life insurance business, retiring as a vice president. Kooser has wryly noted that though both he and Wallace Stevens spent their working lives as insurance executives, Stevens had far more time to write on the job.

Carl Kromminga (b. 1952) is the pastor of New City Church, a multicultural church in Long Beach, California. He and his wife Sandy have five grown children. The composition skills he learned at an early age have been used to write weekly sermons for over 40 years.

Denise Levertov (1923-1997) was an English-born poet, essayist and political activist. At the age of 12, she sent some of her poems to T. S. Eliot, who replied with a two-page letter. At 17 she published her first poem. During World War II, Levertov worked as a nurse at hospitals in the London area. She came to the U.S.in 1948, after marrying American writer Mitchell Goodman. In addition to writing poems, Levertov edited poetry for *The Nation* and *Mother Jones*. She taught at several colleges and universities.

Philip Levine (1928-2015) was born and raised in Detroit, where he began working in auto factories at the age of 14. His poems testify to his passion for ordinary people trapped in poverty and dead end jobs. After earning his BA at Wayne State, he studied at the University of Iowa and Stanford. Levine moved west and spent much of his career teaching at California State University, Fresno. *What Work Is* won the National Book Award in 1991. He was also awarded the Pulitzer Prize for Poetry.

Lou Lipsitz (b. 1939) grew up in Brooklyn, within sight of the night game lights at Ebbets Field. He taught political science at the University of North Carolina for several decades. Now he's a psychotherapist in Chapel Hill, specializing in men's issues, creativity, and life crises. His first book of poems, *Cold Water*, was published in 1967. His other books are *Seeking the Hook* and *If This World Falls Apart*. He plays the harmonica as well as he can. For more, see loulipsitzpoetry.com.

John Logan (1923-1987), a poet, editor, teacher, mentor, and father, was born in Red Oak, Iowa. He earned a BA from Coe College, and did graduate work at Iowa University, Georgetown University, and Notre Dame. Logan produced 14 books of poetry, the first of which was *A Cycle for Mother Cabrini*. His creative works also include a collection of essays, a novel, a play, and nine children. He taught and mentored younger poets at six institutions, the last (for 19 years) the State University of New York at Buffalo.

Marjorie Maddox (b. 1959), Professor of English and Creative Writing at Lock Haven University, has published 11 collections of poetry. These include: *True, False, None of the Above* (Poiema Poetry Series, Illumination Book Award Medalist); *Local News from Someplace Else; Wives' Tales; Transplant, Transport, Transubstantiation* (2004 Yellowglen Prize); and *Perpendicular As I* (Sandstone Book Award). She is also the author of the short story collection *What She Was Saying;* four children's books; *Common Wealth: Contemporary Poets on Pennsylvania* (co-editor); *Presence* (assistant editor); and over 550 stories, essays, and poems in journals and anthologies. For more, see www.marjoriemaddox.com.

Taylor Mali (b. 1965) is the only four-time National Poetry Slam champion and one of the original poets on HBO's "Def Poetry

Jam." The author of five collections of poetry and a book of essays on teaching, he is also the inventor of Metaphor Dice, a game that helps writers think more figuratively. Mali's poems are both accessible and literary. He lives in Brooklyn where he is the founding curator of the Page Meets Stage reading series at the Bowery Poetry Club. For more, see www.taylormali.com.

Edgar Lee Masters (1868-1950) grew up in small-town Illinois, where its citizens and its cemetery were inspirations for his literary work. The most famous, *Spoon River Anthology*, is a collection of more than 200 epitaphs or monologues from the dead—by turns affectionate, caustic, sardonic—in the town cemetery. Only briefly educated, Masters worked in his father's law office, was admitted to the bar, moved to Chicago, and practiced law (for eight years in partnership with Clarence Darrow). Other than the *Anthology*, his 21 books of poetry, and his novels, biographies, and plays are little remembered.

Gail Mazur (b. 1937) is author of seven poetry collections, including *They Can't Take That Away From Me*, finalist for the National Book Award; *Zeppo's First Wife: New and Selected Poems*, winner of the Massachusetts Book Prize and finalist for the *Los Angeles Times* Book Prize; *Figures in a Landscape*; and *Forbidden City*. Her eighth, *Land's End*, is forthcoming in 2020. Mazur grew up in Cambridge, Massachusetts and is a graduate of Smith College. She has taught in the graduate programs of Emerson College, University of Houston, and Boston University. She lives in Provincetown and Cambridge, where she founded the Blacksmith House Poetry Series.

Benjamin Myers (b. 1976) is a former poet laureate of Oklahoma; his most recent book is *Black Sunday: The Dust Bowl Sonnets*. His poems may be read in *The Yale Review*, *Image*, *32 Poems*, *Rattle*, and many other journals. Myers has written essays for publications ranging from *First Things* to *Oklahoma Today*. He teaches literature, writing, and in the Western Civilization Program at Oklahoma Baptist University. For more, see www.benmyers.com.

Marilyn Nelson (b. 1946), a poet, translator, and children's book author, was born in Cleveland, Ohio, the daughter of a school teacher and a U.S. serviceman who was a member of the last graduating class of Tuskegee Airmen. She is the author or translator of more than 20 books and chapbooks for adults and children. Nelson's critically acclaimed books for young adults include, among others, *Carver: A Life in Poems*. She is a professor emerita at the University of Connecticut and the former poet laureate of the state.

Howard Nemerov (1920-1991) was born in New York City into a Russian-Jewish family. He attended the Fieldston School, then studied at Harvard. During World War II, he served as a pilot, first in the Royal Canadian Air Force. After the war Nemerov taught at Hamilton College, then Bennington College, Brandeis, and finally at Washington University in St. Louis, where he was professor and poet in residence for 20 years. Nemerov's poems and novels—witty, ironic, and serious—won major awards. He served twice as poet laureate of the U.S.

Tim Nolan (b. 1954) lives in Minnesota, where he grew up. After graduating from the University of Minnesota, he and his wife

Kate moved to New York City. He earned an MFA degree from Columbia University. Nolan now practices law in Minneapolis, litigating real estate, eminent domain, and construction cases. His favorite place to write, he says, is a comfortable chair in his front yard. Garrison Keillor has read Nolan's poems on "The Writer's Almanac" on NPR. His poems also appear in literary journals.

Joyce Carol Oates (b. 1938) is a novelist, essayist, editor, and poet. Born in Lockport, New York, she earned a BA from Syracuse University, where she graduated valedictorian, and an MA from the University of Wisconsin-Madison. After a year in Texas, she taught at the University of Detroit and subsequently at the University of Windsor in Ontario, and then at Princeton University until 2014. Oates has taught creative writing at UC Berkeley for the past few years. Her list of awards and prizes is almost as lengthy as her astonishingly long list of novels, short stories, essays, and poems.

Sharon Olds (b. 1942), was born in San Francisco, brought up in Berkeley, California and raised, she says, as a "hellfire Calvinist." Attending movies was not permitted, and the family did not own a television. She was sent east to the Dana Hall School in Boston, then educated at Stanford, after which she earned a PhD in English at Columbia. Her poetry is at times autobiographical, dealing directly with memories of abusive parents, and with love, motherhood, sex, and the human condition. Olds teaches at New York University. She has contributed poems to *The New Yorker* for 40 years.

Jan Owen (b.1940) is a South Australian poet and creative writing teacher. Her seventh book, *The Offhand Angel*, was published in 2015. Her volume of translations from Baudelaire's *Les Fleurs du Mal* was published by Arc Publications, and a book of satirical limericks, *The Wicked Flowers of Charles Baudelaire*, came out in 2016. She has received various awards including the Gwen Harwood Poetry Prize and the Philip Hodgins Memorial Medal. Currently she is writing responses to Utagawa Hiroshige's wood block print series "One Hundred Famous Views of Edo."

Linda Pastan (b. 1932) was born to a Jewish family in the Bronx. During her senior year at Radcliffe, she won the *Mademoiselle* poetry prize (Slyvia Plath was the runner-up) and married Ira Pastan, a med student. With two sons launched in school Pastan resumed writing poetry, receiving recognition almost immediately. Her poems, often about family life and relationships, have been widely admired, and her numerous honors include the Dylan Thomas award, the Pushcart Prize, and the Ruth Lily Poetry Prize. Ultimately Pastan produced 15 volumes of poetry, most recently *A Dog Runs Through It*. She was named Maryland poet laureate. She lives in a Washington D.C. suburb.

Theodore Roethke (1908-1963) was among the most influential poets of his generation. He was known as a demanding but beloved teacher. Born in Saginaw, Michigan, he earned BA and MA degrees at the University of Michigan, after which he taught at several colleges, his last 16 years at the University of Washington. He published 10 books of poetry, including *The Waking*, for which he won the Pulitzer Prize, and *The Far Field*.

Roethke, who endured periodic mental breakdowns, is known for his introspective poems.

Carl Sandburg (1878-1967), an American original, left school at 13 and began driving a milk wagon and working in his hometown, Galesburg, Illinois. Sandburg laid bricks, worked on a farm, and rode the rails with hobos before enrolling at Lombard College. He wrote for a Chicago newspaper, then moved to Milwaukee and joined the Socialist Party. He heard America singing in the voices of working class people and saw beauty in the sheen on an oily pond in industrial America. Besides volumes of free verse, he wrote a six-volume biography of Abraham Lincoln and collected and performed folk songs.

David Schelhaas (b. 1942) taught high school English for 23 years and college English for 19 years. He has published two collections of poems, *The God of Material Things* and *Illuminated Manuscript*. Recently he published a memoir, *The Tuning of a Heart*. He and his wife Jerelyn have three children and six grandkids. He is grateful for a wonderful life.

Thomas Schmidt (b. 1939) was once a professor of humanities who now writes poetry in a treehouse perched above a bee-loud glade in Vermont. Since earning a PhD from Cambridge University, he has published quite enough academic books and articles, followed by two novels, dozens of poems, and a pictorial guide to building a chicken coop in the shape of a Model A.

Gary Snyder (b. 1930) is often thought of as a West Coast poet and is associated with the Beats, and with the Pacific

Northwest. Snyder's involvement with Buddhism informs his poetry. His many books include *Myths and Texts*, *The Back Country*, *Turtle Island*, *Ax Handles*, *No Nature: New and Selected Poems*, and *Mountains and Rivers Without End*. Snyder taught at UC Davis from 1986 to 2001. Among his honors, Snyder won the Pulitzer Prize for Poetry, the Bollingen Prize for Poetry, and the Wallace Stevens Award.

Gary Soto (b. 1952) was born in Fresno, California to working-class Mexican-American parents. Growing up, he worked in the fields in the San Joaquin Valley. Soto attended Fresno City College and California State University–Fresno, where he studied with the poet Philip Levine. He earned an MFA degree at UC Irvine. He has published more than 40 books for children, young adults, and adults. Soto was a Young People's Ambassador for the United Farm Workers. He has taught at UC Riverside and UC Berkeley; he now lives in Berkeley.

William Stafford (1914-1993) grew up in Kansas and attended the University of Kansas (BA and MA in English) and earned his PhD at University of Iowa. During World War II he was a conscientious objector and did alternative service at civilian service camps. He moved to the Pacific Northwest and taught at Lewis and Clark College for 32 years. For *Traveling Through the Dark*, Stafford won the National Book Award. Over time he published more than 60 volumes of poetry and prose. In 1970 Stafford was the consultant in poetry to the Library of Congress, the position later known as poet laureate.

James Hercules Sutton (b. 1943) is a graduate of the Boston Latin School, where he was required to take Greek, Latin &

French simultaneously, hence this sonnet. He also graduated from the Iowa Writers' Workshop, where (he says) he learned nothing. These experiences fueled a life-long passion for education reform. After a doctorate in Education Policy, he earned a living as a lobbyist for Iowa's teachers.

Carmen Tafolla (b. 1951) is a native of San Antonio, Texas, where her forebears have lived since the 18th century. Tafolla has published five books of poetry, eight children's books, seven television screenplays, a non-fiction volume, and a collection of short stories. Her one-woman stage show is titled, "My Heart Speaks a Different Language." An alumna of Austin College, Tafollla earned an MA and PhD (in Bilingual and Foreign Education) from the University of Texas. Currently she teaches at UT San Antonio. She was honored as poet laureate of Texas.

Alexandra Teague (b. 1974) was born in Fort Worth, Texas, and grew up in Eureka Springs, Arkansas. She earned her MFA at the University of Florida. Her first book of poetry, *Mortal Geography*, won the Lexi Rudnitsky Prize and the California Book Award. A Stegner Fellow at Stanford and a National Endowment for the Arts Fellow, Teague is an Associate Professor in the University of Idaho's MFA program. She is also co-editor of the anthology *Bullets into Bells: Poets and Citizens Respond to Gun Violence*. For more, see www.alexandrateague.com.

John Updike (1932-2009), an acclaimed and best-selling writer of novels and short stories, achieved celebrity status. He also wrote eight volumes of poetry, much of it witty light verse.

Updike grew up in Shillington, Pennsylvania. His mother wrote novels and short stories; his father taught high school math. *The New Yorker* published one of Updike's poems and one of his stories the same year (1954) he graduated from Harvard. Updike is the author of more than fifty books; his many essays and reviews carried weight in the world of literature and the arts.

Randall VanderMey (b. 1952) earned his MA at the University of Pennsylvania, his MFA in Fiction at the University of Iowa Writer's Workshop, and a PhD at the University of Iowa. Once a student in J. Barry Koops's senior creative writing class at Grand Rapids Christian High, VanderMey went on to a life of writing and teaching at Dordt College, Iowa State, and Westmont College. A lover of words, he has published essays, stories, poems, textbooks, and, more recently, limited edition collections of his iPhone photography. Currently he is revising his second full-length play.

David Wagoner (b. 1926) was born and raised in the midwest (Ohio and Indiana), but when his mentor, Theodore Roethke, called with an offer of a teaching position at University of Washington, he found his true home in the Northwest. Wagoner studied at Penn State and earned an MA from Indiana University. He taught at the University of Washington in Seattle from 1954 to 2002, after which he continued to write, lecture, and edit. In his prolific career he wrote 10 novels and 23 volumes of verse.

Reed Whittemore (1919-2012) was born in Connecticut and attended Phillips Academy. As a sophomore at Yale,

Whittemore and his roommate James Angleton started *Furioso*, one of the famous "little magazines" of its time. Whittemore served as an officer in the Army Air Force during World War II. He spent his 40-year teaching career at Carleton College and University of Maryland. Whittemore published 11 books of poetry and nine of criticism and biography. He was honored as consultant to the Library of Congress—poet laureate—in two decades.

Paul Willis (b. 1955) grew up in Corvallis, Oregon. His passion for teaching and for the forest pushed him to work as a mountain guide in the Cascades. Willis was educated at Wheaton College (Illinois) and earned a PhD at Washington State University. He is a professor of English at Westmont College in Santa Barbara. His most recent collections of poetry are *Deer at Twilight: Poems from the North Cascades* and *Little Rhymes for Lowly Plants*. For more, see www.pauljwillis.com.

David Wright (b. 1966) has written poems, essays, and reviews that have appeared in *32 Poems, Image, Rock & Sling,* and *Spoon River Poetry Review*, among many others. He lives in West Central Illinois where he teaches creative writing and American literature at Monmouth College. He is the author of three poetry collections, including *The Small Books of Bach* and *Local Talent*.

William Butler Yeats (1865-1939) is among the greatest poets to write in the English language. Yeats was born in Protestant Ireland. He lived for 30 years in London, but remained resolutely Irish. The subjects, settings, and characters of his plays and poems are from his homeland, and he was a fierce

Irish nationalist. *The Tower* and *The Wild Swans at Coole* are among Yeats's most highly acclaimed volumes of poems. He received the Nobel Prize for Literature in 1923.

Paul Zimmer (b. 1934) was born in Canton, Ohio. Studying at Kent State University, he was not immediately successful—reportedly he flunked freshman English three times. He was drafted into the U.S. Army, where he read widely and began writing seriously. Zimmer returned to Kent State, and when his first book was published he was awarded the BA degree. He wrote 11 more books of poetry. He has served as the director of university presses in Georgia, Iowa, and Pittsburg and is a founder of the Pitt Poetry Series.

ACKNOWLEDGMENTS

Grateful acknowledgment is made for permission to reprint the following copyrighted works:

Robert Bly, "Gratitude to Old Teachers" from *Eating the Honey of Words: New and Selected Poems* by Robert Bly. Copyright © 1999 by Robert Bly. Reprinted by permission of HarperCollins Publishers.

Gwendolyn Brooks, "We Real Cool" Reprinted by consent of Brooks Permissions.

Sietse Buning, "Hull Humanity" from STYLE AND CLASS by Sietse Buning. Copyright © 1982 by Stanley Wiersma. Reprinted by permission of The Middleburg Press, 105 Kansas Ave., Orange City, IA 51041. Telephone: 712-737-4198.

Herm Card, "Between the Lines" by Herm Card. Copyright © 1998 by Herm Card. Reprinted by permission of the author.

Brenda Cárdenas, "Lecciones de Lengua" from *Boomerang* by Brenda Cárdenas. Copyright © 2009 Bilingual Press/Editorial Bilingüe. Reprinted by permission of Bilingual Press/Editorial Bilingüe, Arizona State University, Tempe, AZ.

Charles Causley, "Timothy Winters" from *Collected Poems* 1951-2000 by Charles Causley. Copyright © 1970 by Charles Causley. Reprinted by permission of David Higham Associates, Limited.

Brian Doyle, "Poem for a Son Going Off to College" from *How the Light Gets In* by Brian Doyle. Copyright © 2001 by Brian Doyle. Reprinted by permission of Orbis Books.

Stephen Dunn, "On the Death of a Colleague" from *Landscape at the Edge of the Century* by Stephen Dunn. Copyright © 1991 by Stephen Dunn. Used by permission of W. W. Norton & Company, Inc. "The Sacred" from *Between Angels* by Stephen Dunn. Copyright © 1989 by Stephen Dunn. Used by permission of W. W. Norton & Company, Inc.

Maura Eichner, "What My Teachers Taught Me I Try to Teach My Students" from *Hope is a Blind Bard* by Maura Eichner. Copyright © 2000 by Maura Eichner. Reprinted by permission of the School Sisters of Notre Dame of the Atlantic-Midwest Province.

Louise Erdrich, "Indian Boarding School: The Runaways" from *Original Fire: Selected and New Poems* by Louise Erdrich. Copyright © 2003 by Louise Erdrich. Reprinted by permission of HarperCollins Publishers.

Peter Everwine, "Lessons" from *Listening Long and Late* by Peter Everwine. Copyright © 2013. Reprinted by permission of the University of Pittsburgh Press.

Jane Flanders, "The Geography of Children" from *Timepiece*, by Jane Flanders. Copyright © 1988. Reprinted by permission of the University of Pittsburgh Press.

permission of the University of Illinois Press.